Happy New Year?

It's 12.17 am on January 1st, 2009. I'm Emily Hausmann. I'm from Berlin and I go to Chalk Farm School for Girls in London but, listen, **never mind** that now! **None** of that is important. The important thing right now is that I'm *alive!* I have ***actually*** *survived* Christmas with my crazy German-English family! I feel a bit like one of those people who walks away from a plane crash with only a broken fingernail. Hallelujah!

I had been so sure that our first Christmas at my grandmother's house in *years* would be a bizarre kind of **bilingual** disaster movie: *Massaker at Christmas* or something. But it's been totally peaceful. One big, long *Stille Nacht*. It's a **miracle**. It's enough to make you really believe in the magic of Christmas.

Not really. It wasn't Santa Claus or any of his **elves** who made it possible for us all to be together under one roof. It was my mother. She had **plainly** told my dad that she would **divorce** him if he complained about *anything* at Grandma's. Dad hasn't opened his mouth all holiday.

+++ never mind – *hier:* kümmer dich nicht drum +++ none – nichts, kein +++ actually – sogar, tatsächlich +++ bilingual – zweisprachig +++ miracle – Wunder +++ elf – Elfe +++ plain – deutlich +++ to divorce s.o. – sich von jmdm. scheiden lassen +++

We've just done everything *nach der feinen englischen Art.* We played by the Queen Mother's – my grandma's – rules. We opened our presents on the 25th (Not on the 24th). We ate **turkey**, not **goose**. And my father *said nothing.*

Right now, it's **New Year's Eve** and we're all just sitting around; Dad, Mum, Grandma, my Auntie Nora and me. My little brother Max has just gone to bed. We've all finished saying: *Happy New Year!* and remembering not to try and kiss my grandmother, who hates kissing.

The adults are now all **sipping** sherry and talking politely about the world economic crisis: *will be a difficult year,* ***bankruptcy****, blah blah.* Whatever. I'm not thinking about the **stock markets** crashing. I'm thinking about Sam. Sam Reid, my boyfriend, world's nicest guy! I can almost *see* him.

No, I'm not mad. Grandma's TV is on in the background. It's probably the world's smallest television and about the size of a packet of **fish fingers**. But if I stare hard enough I can see lots of drunk, cold people celebrating on its tiny screen. *Edinburgh!* a little voice says. *Hogmanay, the Scottish New Year, is famous and Edinburgh has one of the biggest street parties anywhere.*

Sam's *there, right now,* at that street party! His mobile hasn't been working, but he still managed to send me a message from a friend's phone about half an hour ago: *Edinburgh cold cold cold, but you are hot hot hot all the best for 2009.xxxxx.* Hmm. No one's ever called me *hot hot hot* before. I could get used to it.

+++ turkey – Truthahn +++ goose – Gans +++ New Year's Eve – Silvester +++ to sip – nippen +++ bankruptcy – Bankrott, Konkurs +++ stock market – Börse +++ fish finger – Fischstäbchen +++

It looks like a beautiful place, Edinburgh. There's the castle, set high above the city, spectacular fireworks exploding above it. "Sehr schön," says my father suddenly. He's talking to me, of course, the only other German in the room. "Edinburgh ist wie Rom, wusstest du das? Sieben Hügel. Wir müssen da unbedingt irgendwann hin."

Then he looks **in disgust** at the sickly sweet glass of sherry in his hand and **mutters** to my grandmother, "Mrs Millington, do you have any whisky in the house?"

My grandmother **nods**. She has a dangerously dreamy look on her face. I know that look! It's a *nostalgic* one. Oh no! I hear the Queen Mother say, "I remember the **bombers**, how scared we were …" My grandmother is about to start telling one of her legendary World War II anecdotes. She has never really forgiven

+++ in disgust – angeekelt +++ to mutter – murmeln +++ to nod – nicken +++ bomber – Kampfflugzeug +++

the Germans for bombing her and her friends and family. Strange.

Dad, who's just fetched himself a glass of whisky the size of Edinburgh Castle, **winks** at me. It's the signal: *Evakuieren!!* He's right: when Grandma starts talking about the war, it's a bad time to be German. It's a bad time to be *half* German, like me. *Los!*

Back in the safety of my room, I sit down on my bed and **sigh**. I'm looking at the Christmas present Sam gave me, a beautiful book of black and white photographs of Scotland. I **keep** reading what he's written inside the front cover: *I hope 2009 is the year I can show you round my home country!* Wow.

I keep thinking, too, about how Sam gave me this book. We'd had a fight – after a disaster at the Bloomsbury Christmas party when my **archenemy** Cyclops Dobson tried to get her **claws** into him. I'd left the party with my heart breaking. I really did think that Sam might actually have enjoyed Cyclops flirting with him. I really did think that Sam and me might not make it into 2009 as a couple.

We did, **though**. Just as I was about to leave Chalk Farm for the holidays, Sam appeared to give me not only my beautiful present but two of the best pieces of news I've ever had: firstly, that he wasn't interested in Cyclops, and secondly, that he was, in fact, totally interested in

+++ to wink at – zuzwinkern +++ to sigh – seufzen +++ to keep doing sth. – etw. immer weiter tun +++ archenemy – Erzfeind/in +++ claw – Klaue, Kralle +++ though – trotzdem +++

me. I was so happy. I was ecstatic. Everything's cool, isn't it? So why do I still feel so ***uneasy***?

I think I **trust** Sam. I *think* I do. I mean, you never know. I *think* I believe that nothing happened with Cyclops at the party. I haven't known Sam very long and you can be wrong about someone but I'm about 87.6% sure that he's not interested in Cyclops. No, it's not that that's making me uneasy. Not really.

There are other reasons, two of them. And both of them have to do with the – what's the expression in English again? *Haar in der Suppe* – fly in the **ointment**, that's it! The fly in the ointment *of my life* – Miss Bardwell.

Ms Bardwell is my Latin teacher and **housemistress** at Chalk Farm School, in case you didn't know. She hates me, in case you didn't know. And as my family certainly now do know, thanks to my **report card** from last term.

My report card. I had nearly forgotten about it, I'll be honest. Miss Bardwell had handed them out at the Kensington Christmas party and I had remembered to stick mine in my suitcase to bring here. Honest. But so much had happened over Christmas that *actually getting it out to show my parents* just went totally out of my head.

Luckily, it didn't go out of my grandmother's. On the 28th of December, as we were all laying around the living room lazily, the Queen Mother suddenly woke up from a **nap** in front of the fire and looked at me closely:

+++ uneasy – unbehaglich +++ to trust – vertrauen +++ ointment – Salbe +++ housemistress – Hausvorsteherin +++ report card – Zeugnis +++ nap – Nickerchen +++

"Shouldn't you have had your first report card by now, Emily?"

Grandma had probably been having a bad dream. Maybe her bad dream went something like this – she'd paid a **fortune** for her granddaughter to go to an expensive boarding school in London and her granddaughter had **messed up** her chance. "Oh, I'll get it later, Grandma," I said, trying to seem relaxed.

But my mother was listening, too, by now. She's a teacher and so has a radar for this **stuff**. She just said, calmly, "Emily, I'd actually really like to see it *now*, if you don't mind. **No point in** waiting."

No way out. So I **headed** upstairs, found my case and took out the two envelopes hiding at the bottom of it: *Report Card, Emily Hausmann, Third form, Chalk Farm School for Girls.*

I opened my copy first. I didn't want to be unpleasantly surprised. I took a breath so deep I could feel it in my **toenails** and read.

I knew my grades already. They were OK, mainly "B"s, one "A" for Art – hurrah! – and, OK, OK, a couple of "C"s. I was only really worried about two things: what Mr Benn and Miss Bardwell would have to say about me. I read Mr Benn's comment first. Mr Benn's my English Literature teacher and I had a bad start with him when I handed in a "copy" of Olga Petrova's essay to him. But he's a nice man, Mr Benn, thankfully: *After*

+++ fortune – Vermögen +++ to mess up – vermasseln +++ stuff – Sachen +++ no point in – kein Grund zu +++ to head – *hier:* gehen +++ toenail – Zehennagel +++

some **initial hiccups***, Emily has made excellent progress.* Phew.

Then I said a silent **prayer** and read Miss Bardwell's comment. It's as long as a Russian novel – she gets most space, as my housemistress. And it's as depressing as most Russian novels. It says things like this:

Emily has had a very disappointing first term at Chalk Farm School. She still has to learn traditional English **values** *such as tolerance of others and team* **spirit***. She has also spent far too much time "***socialising***" with several pupils from St Dougan's boy school. Emily needs to come back after Christmas* **suitably** *re-focussed if she is to really get the most out of her year at Chalk Farm School for Girls.*

Miss Bardwell says other things, too, about me: *ignoring rules about school uniform* – once! –*showing no interest at all in sports* – is that really so bad? – and other stuff that I don't want to remember, thanks.

I didn't cry. I didn't. But I was hurt and **embarrassed.** *Several* members of St Dougan's – that makes me sound like a total **tart**! It was only *two pupils*! Just Sam and Ed Stanton, Sam's bandmate. And he **dumped** me after five minutes so I didn't exactly "socialise" with him for very long.

I went back down the stairs to the living room, where

+++ initial – anfänglich +++ hiccup – *hier:* Problemchen +++ prayer – Gebet +++ value – Wert +++ spirit – Geist +++ to socialise – Kontakte knüpfen +++ suitable – angemessen +++ to be embarrassed – sich schämen +++ tart – Flittchen +++ to dump s.o. – mit jmdm. Schluss machen +++

everyone was waiting for me. *Dead girl walking.* I was scared stiff about what my parents would say.

The strange thing was, in fact, that Mum and Dad didn't go crazy when they read it. I had thought they would hit me with the Queen Mother's **fire iron** or order me to go to a **convent** school in Switzerland but they didn't. (The Queen Mother did go for another very, very long lie down after she'd seen it, however.)

My mother just looked **puzzled** and said, "Well, that's *odd.* I mean, your grades are OK. The comments from most teachers are good and yet your housemistress says it's all terrible. I'm afraid I don't see why."

Then she looked at me thoughtfully. "Maybe the best thing is for me to get in touch with Miss Bardwell to talk about ..."

I **gasped** *no!* and my mum just laughed. "You're not scared of her, are you?"

"No," I **mumbled**. You shouldn't lie to your parents, of course. Obviously, I am more scared of Miss Bardwell than I am of anything else in the universe.

I don't really understand quite *why* Miss Bardwell hates me so much. But I do know that one of the reasons is Auntie Nora. Auntie Nora and Miss Bardwell were at Chalk Farm School together years ago, and they were **sworn** enemies then. Everyone tells me that I'm like Nora, which is generally great because Nora is cool and a brilliant photographer, something I'd love to be. The only time it's not great being like her is when Miss

+++ fire iron – Feuerzange +++ convent – Kloster +++ puzzled – verwundert +++ to gasp – nach Luft schnappen +++ to mumble – murmeln, nuscheln +++ sworn – eingeschworen +++

Bardwell's around. Like at the Kensington Christmas party, **for instance.**

That party is actually the other reason I'm a big **bag of nerves** right now. It was there that I discovered that Auntie Nora was actually the old flame of Miss Bardwell's **fiancé, aka** Sam's Chemistry teacher at St Dougan's Boys' School aka Mr Michaels, our party "Santa". I found this out the hard way: Nora kissed "Santa" and Santa chased Nora. Something tells me Miss Bardwell wasn't too excited about this.

Nora hasn't said a word to me about Mr Michaels all holiday. But every time her mobile has rung, I've jumped. What if she's having an affair with "Ben" Michaels? I have to get Nora by herself tomorrow and find out what's going on.

Finally I fall asleep, still holding Sam's present. **Tight.**

+++ for instance – zum Beispiel +++ bag of nerves – Nervenbündel +++ fiancé(e) – Verlobte/r +++ aka – alias +++ tight – fest +++

Death Wish

It's the next day, the afternoon, and everyone is in the dining room. Max, Dad and Nora are playing some "spooky" 3-D **haunted house** game that Max got for Christmas. Mum is doing more "humanitarian work", looking at photo albums with the Queen Mother. I'm wandering about restlessly, picking up books and putting them down again a lot. I'm really only thinking about how to talk to Nora alone. Finally I say in a **casual** voice, "Anyone **fancy** getting a bit of fresh air with me?"

Everyone looks at me, shocked. I am not known in my family, I'll be honest, for my love of "fresh air". I stare hard at Nora, hoping that she'll pick up my signal. Luckily, she's a **genius** and she does. She smiles and then winks at me and says, "Oh right, *fresh air*. Let's go for a walk into the village, shall we?"

I look outside and sigh. It's about minus **34 degrees** in Surrey right now. But it's also our last chance to talk *woman to woman*. Nora's a photographer for a big newspaper and she's off to Beirut this week on a "long **assignment**". She's so relaxed about it. I'm more worried about

+++ haunted house – Haus, in dem es spukt +++ casual – beiläufig +++ to fancy – Lust haben +++ genius – Genie +++ 34 degrees (Fahrenheit) = ca. 1–2 Grad Celsius +++ assignment – Auftrag +++

going back to Chalk Farm than she is about going to the Middle East. That says it all.

Nora and me **head off** to **stomp** around the village nearest Grandma's house. Actually, I hate the village. There's only one small shop open and everything is deserted. I'm a city girl. I like to have people around. I like to think that if I get attacked by a psychopath, someone will hear me scream. Here, no one would hear you – except Nora, of course. She'd hear me. And she's waiting to hear what I have to say now.

OK, I'll **get the ball rolling** by telling her about Sam, I decide. She must be curious about him – she saw us disappear behind the school together when she came to pick me up at Christmas. If I open my heart to her about Sam, then she might feel like she has to explain what's happening with Mr Michaels. Brilliant plan, eh? So I talk and talk about my perfect boyfriend. *Great guy. Wonderful drummer. Scottish. Funny.* It's all a bit embarrassing, really.

When I've finished telling her everything I can think of to tell her about Sam, Nora smiles.

"He sounds lovely," she says. Then she smiles again. This time it's a different kind of smile. A bit **naughty**.

"Dating is a nightmare at a girls' school, isn't it?" she giggles. "I remember how frustrating it was – there's never any privacy. All that kissing on park benches used to drive me *crazy*."

"Yes," I say, a bit uncertainly. I'm not sure where this

+++ to head off – losziehen +++ to stomp – stapfen +++ to get the ball rolling – den Ball ins Rollen bringen +++ naughty – frech +++

conversation is leading. Nora's right, of course. At Chalk Farm School, there's both zero privacy and high security. St Dougan's boys' lives are at risk if they go anywhere near us. It would probably have been easier for my dad to have popped over from East Berlin in the 80s to visit Mum in England than it is for Sam to visit me at Chalk Farm in 2009. Well, almost. Dad probably wouldn't agree.

Then Nora does something wonderful. "Look, I'm going to be away for a month or so now. I probably should have done this a while ago."

She reaches into the pocket of her lovely coat – a Prada one, I'm a bit ***obsessed*** with it – pulls out a key and hands it to me. "This is for my flat. Somewhere you can be by yourselves." Nora smiles another **wicked** smile. "And of course, Emily Hausmann, I'm trusting you. No wild parties. And no, *you know*. None of that."

I **blush**. It's brilliant, of course. A **haven**. I hold the key to 17 Cleveland Street, **Fitzrovia, W1** in the palm of my hand for a second, just enjoying the warm feeling of freedom that it gives me. And the fact that it now means I have somewhere to talk to Sam without Cyclops/Mrs White/crowds of tourists/Miss Bardwell listening to me.

Miss Bardwell, *hmmmm.* I don't really want to but I *have to* ask about Mr Michaels. Time is **running out**: we can almost see The Grange, Grandma's house, from here. It's just behind those bushes, the scary ones, where

+++ to be obsessed – besessen sein +++ wicked – schelmisch +++ to blush – rot werden +++ haven – Hafen, Zufluchtsort +++ Fitzrovia W1 – Stadtteil von London +++ to run out – ablaufen +++

I always think someone's going to jump out at me – *Stop it! Ask her!*

I try to bring the subject up **gently:** *"Hey, did you and Ben have a nice time in White Out after the party?"* But it's **obvious at once** that Nora really doesn't want to talk about it. "We're just friends," says Nora sharply. "Honestly, I wouldn't do that to you. Or to Miss Bardwell."

"He's interested in you, right?" I ask. I really want Nora to say: *Wrong. Miss Bardwell is his one and only love. Please.*

But Nora says nothing. She looks a bit sad. "Let's just get back, I'm freezing."

I now have a key at least. And by the time Nora and me get back, my mother has a plan. Having reflected on my report card all week, she has a surprise for me. She secretly called Miss Bardwell, it seems – **yikes**! – and they agreed to meet at Chalk Farm to discuss my "progress". Mum has changed her travel arrangements and will now come to London with Nora and me.

Mum tells me all this like it's ***no big deal*** but I know that it is. It will cost her time and money she doesn't have. Worse than that, she'll have to miss the flight back to Berlin she was **supposed to** be on with Dad and Max and fly by herself. She hates flying, my mum, and she *really* hates flying by herself. A mother's love, eh?

So we say *Auf Wiedersehen!* to Max and Dad the next day, with my dad making lots of totally uncool jokes

+++ gentle – *hier:* vorsichtig +++ obvious – offensichtlich +++ at once – sofort +++ Yikes! – Huch! +++ no big deal – kein Problem +++ to be supposed to – sollen +++

about me staying away from boys. Then we have one last "girls only" day – lots of sherry, lots of photo albums – at The Grange before Nora, Mum and me have to leave.

We say goodbye to the Queen Mother, who tries very hard to look sad and says things like: *Oh no! I'm all alone again!* but who I think is secretly *ecstatic* that we're all finally going. I can tell that Nora and the Queen Mother are both **exhausted** from being polite and kind to each other for so long.

Grandma gives me a firm handshake with – hurrah! – a 50-pound note in it! As I try to thank her, she just leans over and whispers in my ear, "Thank me by trying harder this term, Emily." Humph. **Annoying.**

Mum, Nora and me then start the drive back to Chalk Farm. No one says much on the way – everyone's in quite a serious mood. Nora's mind is in the Middle East, I'm pretty sure. Mum's is in Berlin, she'll catch a flight there tonight. My thoughts are with Sam, of course. I wonder where he is right now. Is he back in London already? Or **en route** from Scotland?

As we near the school, I'm starting to get nervous. Nora's car is a little bit of **vintage** heaven (a 1973 Citroën) but it would have been faster to walk from The Grange. My mother has an **appointment** with Miss Bardwell in her office at 11 o'clock. If we're late, Miss Bardwell will come downstairs and look for us – I know her. If she goes downstairs, she'll see Nora. I don't want any blood **spilled.** Especially not mine.

+++ exhausted – erschöpft +++ annoying – nervig +++ en route (frz.) – auf dem Weg +++ vintage – retro +++ appointment – Verabredung +++ to spill – vergießen +++

But it is indeed 11.17 am as we arrive at Chalk Farm School. My worst **nightmare** has come true: Miss Bardwell really is standing on the front steps of the school. She's spotted us now, of course – you can't miss Nora's car. It looks like something *Tim und Struppi* would drive around in.

As Nora parks, I can't take my eyes off Miss Bardwell. The strange thing is that even though she's seen us, she hasn't *seen us,* if you know what I mean. Normally she looks like thunder whenever Nora or I are within 3.5 metres of her but now her **expression** is totally **blank**. There's nothing, no emotion of any kind.

Nora should escape while she still can! I get out of the car quickly. "Well, thanks!" I say to my aunt. My aunt whom I *love. Please don't get out!* "We'll get my bags – you're in a hurry."

But Nora just smiles. "No, I'll help you. And I'd like to say hello to Connie, wish her a Happy New Year!"

"Connie" is Miss Bardwell and my aunt has a death wish. She works in places like Beirut and Afghanistan and *after kissing Santa at the Kensington Christmas party, she now wants to say "hello" to Miss Bardwell.* Like it *never happened.* Like Miss Bardwell will just have *forgotten.*

I get my bag from the **boot**. I can feel a big **vein tensing** in my head as I watch my mother shaking hands with Miss Bardwell: "Hello, I'm Eleanor Hausmann, Emily's …"

+++ nightmare – Albtraum +++ expression – *hier:* Gesichtsausdruck +++ blank – leer +++ boot – Kofferraum +++ vein – Ader +++ to tense – *hier:* pulsieren +++

Miss Bardwell interrupts her, "I know." Of course she does. My mother was a few years above her at school. But again, it's strange. Miss Bardwell's normally as **acid** as the **vinegar** I love to put on my chips here in England. Now her voice just sounds flat. Then it's my turn to greet Miss Bardwell and as I do so, I see her face up close.

She's been crying. I'm absolutely certain of it. Crying for *days.* Miss Bardwell's eyes are totally dried out and are no longer full of evil – they just look like **sultanas** baked in the sun too long. Nora's now standing right next to her and trying to say hello. There's still nothing from Miss Bardwell. Zero response.

Oohh, it's *scary.* The calm before the storm, it must be.

As Mum and me walk Nora back to her car, I keep waiting for Miss Bardwell to **whip** a knife out from under her Batman **cloak** and throw it into our backs.

I'm getting a really bad feeling about all this.

All I can do is pray that I'm wrong. Maybe Miss Bardwell's not been crying for the whole holiday because of Mr Michaels. Maybe she's just sad because she got a toga in the wrong size for Christmas or something?

My mother and me say goodbye to Nora, who keeps looking over **guiltily** at Miss Bardwell. I make a bad joke: *I'll* ***campaign*** *for you if you're kidnapped!* and Nora *almost* laughs. Then it's time. Mum and me go up to Miss Bardwell's office. Mum and Miss Bardwell will talk

+++ acid – sauer +++ vinegar – Essig +++ sultana – Sultanine +++ to whip – *hier:* plötzlich hervorziehen +++ cloak – Mantel +++ guilty – schuldbewusst +++ to campaign – sich einsetzen kämpfen +++

in private first. I'm to wait outside on "**Death Row**", on the chairs lined up in front of Miss Bardwell's office. They'll call me in when they're ready.

It's horrible sitting here, actually. You can ***sort of*** hear what's being said if you try. I don't want to try. I can just imagine: *Emily: boy hungry.* ***Slacker.*** *Loser.* I have my iPod with me and I stick that on to block it all out.

I'm halfway through Vampire Weekend when Mum and Miss Bardwell come out. They both look calm. No **bruises** or any other wounds. My mother says **briskly**, "Miss Bardwell and I have had a long discussion about you, Emily." Miss Bardwell nods and **smoothes down** her skirt. "I have said everything I wanted to say to your mother, Emily. There's no need for us to talk."

+++ Death Row – Todestrakt +++ sort of – irgendwie +++ slacker – Faulenzer/in, Nichtstuer/in +++ bruise – Bluterguss +++ wound – Wunde +++ brisk – rasch +++ to smooth down – glatt streichen +++

I'm totally confused. Have I just been **expelled**??? I try to imagine my old English teacher Herr Eisenhardt's face if I came back to the Hermann-Hesse-Gymnasium six months early: *Ich wurde von der Schule verwiesen.* It would be *sort of* cool, of course. *Ja, ich war einfach zu viel mit Jungs beschäftigt!*

If this is goodbye from Miss Bardwell, then it's a short one. She just shakes my hand – again, the same empty **gaze** – and shuts the door of her office, leaving me with my mouth hanging open. I'd love to have seen if the picture of Mr Michaels she always has on her desk was still there but she's too fast.

I look at my mother, who just **shrugs her shoulders**. "It wasn't exactly what I was expecting. I asked Miss Bardwell about your report card – why it was so bad when your grades were actually OK. She just said straight away that she had probably been too hard on you. She did say you could concentrate more in class, though." My mother gives me one of her I-may-be-your-mother-but-I-am-also-a-teacher-stares.

"She said all that??" I gasp. Everything is going round and round. The school is spinning. It's like being in the "Wizard of Oz", in the middle of the **cyclone**.

My mother nods. "I don't think her mind is totally on her job, to be honest. She seemed *sad*. Any idea why?"

Mum doesn't know what happened between Nora and Mr Michaels. She'd go crazy if she found out, I'm fairly sure. I think Nora was fairly sure, too, which is why

+++ to expel – rauswerfen +++ gaze – Blick +++ to shrug one's shoulders – mit den Schultern zucken +++ cyclone – Wirbelsturm +++

she didn't tell Mum. So I just shrug my shoulders and mumble something about the time of year: *maybe she's got a cold? A stomach virus?*

Mum has to go. The last thing she says to me is: *Be kind to her.* Then she rushes off, trying to **pretend** she's not about to have a **nervous breakdown** at the airport. I just hope she doesn't attack the air hostess like that time – oh, never mind. Mum would kill me if I told you about that.

+++ to pretend – so tun als ob +++ nervous breakdown – Nervenzusammenbruch +++

There Must Be an Angel

Me be kind to Miss Bardwell? Everything is completely crazy at the moment. Miss Bardwell and Mr Michaels must have **split up**. If they have, then *everyone* at both Chalk Farm and St Dougan's schools will know about it soon. **That sucks**, of course. Miss Bardwell will die of shame. I remember how I felt about Ed Stanton …

I suddenly realise I am experiencing ***empathy*** with Miss Bardwell. A large pig flies past the window outside and waves at me. The pig is holding a sign that says, "All you need is love" and wearing a pair of Cyclops' sunglasses.

The other emotion I'm experiencing right now is *fear.* Miss Bardwell is clearly in some kind of **weird** love-shock-coma now. And when she wakes up, she'll remember that she hates me, right?

For the moment though, it seems there's now a **guardian angel** watching over me at Chalk Farm School. And he or she has been busy: when I arrive at my **dorm**, 3B, only Becks and Melissa, my nice roommates, are there. They can't wait to tell me the good news: Amanda

+++ to split up – sich trennen +++ That sucks – Das ist ätzend +++ empathy – Mitgefühl +++ weird – komisch +++ guardian angel – Schutzengel +++ dorm – Schlafsaal +++

and her family missed their flight from Bangkok yesterday! Cyclops won't be back till later in the week. Hurrah!

This is fantastic. I relax totally. It gives me a chance to chat in peace to Melissa and Becks about their Christmas breaks. Becks had a perfect "holiday": non-stop action, it seems, rock climbing and snowboarding in France. "A *total* adrenaline kick. We had at least two **avalanches**." It sounds like my ultimate *nightmare* holiday. I mean, what's a holiday for if not to *relax*?

Melissa's less enthusiastic about Christmas. "It was OK," she says quietly. "I did a lot with Almonds, you know, some brilliant riding. But ..." She **hesitates**. "My parents had a few fights with Josh."

Of course! With all my private drama I'd almost forgotten about the other shock from the Kensington Christmas party. Olga, our ex-roommate, Melissa's ex-best friend and possibly ex-girlfriend of her brother – a lot of exes in there, I'm sorry – told us she was leaving school to go back to sunny Florida. She's basically "**engaged**" to Taki, it seems, some **handsome** millionaire's son: it must be hell. Seriously, it probably is.

Melissa looks really sad: "Josh is heartbroken about Olga. He thinks she's being sold into *slavery* or something. He wanted to fly to Florida to 'help' her. He asked my parents for money to go there and he went crazy when they wouldn't give it to him. Oh, Emily, it was *terrible*."

Melissa's had one e-mail from Olga since she arrived

+++ avalanche – Lawine +++ to hesitate – zögern +++ engaged – verlobt +++ handsome – gut aussehend +++

back in America: "She's even got a secret e-mail account and she uses Internet cafés in case 'they' look at her computer! It's all really strange. But she's OK, she says. She'll ..."

"... survive," I finish. Olga's a survivor. I hope.

"But as for Josh ..." Melissa shrugs. "It's going to take time."

Melissa and Becks then listen politely to me talking about Grandma's excellent Christmas turkey and German-English relations at The Grange but I can see what they *really* want is hot **gossip** about Nora and Mr Michaels. Nora kissing Mr Michaels must be the talk of the school! But I must be **discreet**. I *must.*

When I don't give them what they want, Becks tries **fishing**: "We saw Miss Bardwell this morning and she seemed awfully *depressed.* She didn't even look at us. We were wondering if, you know ..."

Becks gazes at me meaningfully. For once, though, my lips are **sealed**. Anyway, I'm just as much in the dark as they are.

Our Latin class on Monday morning confirms it – Miss Bardwell is a new woman. She doesn't make fun of me or Sadie or any of the other girls she doesn't like. She doesn't make super-**lame** jokes about Julius Caesar's haircut or anything. She just goes through the work and then *ten minutes before class is* ***due to*** *finish* says briskly, "I think we'll just stop there for today, girls." Everyone

+++ gossip – Klatsch und Tratsch +++ discreet – verschwiegen +++ to fish – *hier:* herauskitzeln +++ to seal – versiegeln +++ lame – lahm +++ to be due to – sollen +++

gasps. Miss Bardwell has *never* before finished a class one nanosecond before it should end.

I'm really sorry about the reason for this change in personality, of course, but it's still *brilliant.* Having no Amanda around is **the icing on the cake. Yummy**. I'll have another piece of my new life, thanks.

All in all, it's just an incredibly pleasant first day back at school. For me at least. A lot of the girls are, in fact, really sad: Mr Radcliffe, our young, **gorgeous supply teacher** for Art, has left. Sadie's hysterical – you'd think he was *dead.*

I'm **thrilled**, of course. It means Miss Shaw, our real Art teacher, is back! Her broken arm isn't broken any more! I **rush off** to see her that afternoon. I suddenly remember that I still have the darkroom key I "borrowed" last term. Miss Shaw looks well, though her arm is **stiff**, she says. She laughs when I try to give her the darkroom key back: "Listen, Emily, why don't you just hold on to it? That way you can use the darkroom whenever you want to."

How does the song go? Sing it with me now: *Oh, it's **such** a perfect day!* It's almost too good to be true. Now all I need is one phone call from across the street. My guardian angel waves his/her wand and *ping!* I hear my new ringtone – *Ring of Fire* by Johnny Cash. (A classic, all right?)

I recognise the number. How could I not? It's Sam's

+++ the icing on the cake – das Beste +++ yummy – lecker +++ gorgeous – wunderschön +++ supply teacher– Aushilfslehrer/in +++ thrilled – begeistert +++ to rush off – wegeilen +++ stiff – steif +++ such – solch +++

mobile! I wonder how long it's been "working" again. My heart **beats** just a little bit faster as I hear his voice wishing me a Happy New Year. He sounds ill and he is: "I've got a cold," he **coughs**, "Hogmanay was *arctic*." Then his voice drops a bit; I can **hardly** hear him. "Listen, a few things happened over Christmas that we really need to talk about. If you can give me a couple of days to get my voice back, that'd be great. What about the weekend?"

Oh no. A few things happened? Like what? *I kissed an amazing blonde at the street party, Emily. Cyclops just happened to pass through Edinburgh on her way to Bangkok and, well, we fell madly in love.*

Then Sam says, "Emily, are you still there?" I was lost for a moment, it's true. Just when I thought things were about to **settle down**: what is it *now*? Sam had been **behaving** a bit strangely before Christmas, it's true. He seemed a bit **distracted**, a bit **moody**. I'd sort of forgotten. *Concentrate.* I can just ***sense*** that Sam is about to suggest that we meet in White Out. I've got a better location for us now, of course – Nora's place. As quick as a flash, I say, "If I text you an address, can you meet me there on Saturday at 6ish?" And then I hang up. Emily Hausmann, International Woman of Mystery.

I call Maudie after I've spoken to Sam. I can't wait to tell her and Kim about Nora's place. We have a party location! Oops, sorry – a *study* location. (No parties,

+++ to beat – schlagen +++ to cough – husten +++ hardly – kaum +++ to settle down – sich beruhigen +++ to behave – sich verhalten +++ distracted – abgelenkt +++ moody – launisch +++ to sense – merken, spüren +++

Nora said, remember?) Actually, I *really* can't wait to "study": I invite the girls over to Fitzrovia on Friday. I've planned the whole weekend already. I'll see Maudie and Kim on Friday, Sam on Saturday. And if Sam dumps me on Saturday night, then I can just move into Nora's for a month and cry.

He can't be thinking about dumping me, can he? I mean, he hasn't even seen me since Christmas, so I can't have done anything to make him have changed his mind about me. Can I?

I try to take my mind off *things that happened over Christmas* by planning "something special" for the weekend. I could make dinner for everyone. I mean, I've never actually **hosted** a dinner party before in my life, but it can't be that difficult, can it? I've seen that *Das*

+++ to host – veranstalten +++

Perfekte Promi-Dinner programme: some of those "Promis" are so stupid that if they had another brain cell it would be lonely. If *they can* manage to cook dinner …

A brilliant plan is taking its brilliant place in my brilliant mind and it goes like this: I'll prepare an amazing meal for the girls on Friday. If, as I **suspect**, I'm a natural talent at cooking, then *maybe* I'll risk making dinner for Sam on Saturday. *Liebe geht durch den Magen*, as my father likes to say, usually as my mother orders our second takeaway pizza of the week.

I spend ages looking up dinner parties on the Internet. A theme would be good. Asian? **Mediterranean**? Spanish would be *muy bueno*. I can just see us all sitting at Nora's **oak** table, eating paella and olives. Maudie/Kim/Sam looking at me in amazement: *Emily, this is delicious. We had no idea you could cook.*

Paella must be easy, eh? A bit of rice and fish: **chop**, chop, **boil**, boil. Then I find a recipe for paella and **the bubble bursts**. It's an absolute *nightmare*. I'd have to take the whole day off school on Friday to fly to Valencia and get all the **ingredients** for one thing. Any of you heard of sofrito? No, I didn't think so.

I'm feeling a bit depressed about how *complicated* cooking actually is when I remember that – hey! – this is Britain, the home of the *Fertiggericht*! *No one* actually cooks here, Nora once told me. She also gave me a tip –

+++ to suspect – vermuten +++ mediterranean – mediterran, südländisch +++ oak – Eiche +++ to chop – zerkleinern +++ to boil – kochen +++ the bubble bursts – die Seifenblase platzt +++ ingredient – Zutat +++

the name of a **posh**, expensive supermarket which does the *best* ready made meals. Voilà.

That's all settled then. *One perfect dinner party* ***to go*** *please*! There is still, however, just one *tiny* **obstacle** standing between me and my new dream life as the perfect hostess. If I am to be away from the school overnight at the weekend, then I need permission from my housemistress. So I have to ask Miss Bardwell if I can stay at *Nora's*. At her *arch-rival's*. Yikes.

But when I go to see her in her office on Thursday, Miss Bardwell just says: *Yes, you may go, Emily,* in a flat, empty voice. No questions asked. I have the feeling, in fact, that I could have asked her for anything: *Can I stop wearing my uniform, Miss? Can I invite Sam over to the dorm, Miss? Can I kick Cyclops out of Chalk Farm School, Miss?* I don't. I just run for my life instead.

I do give myself just enough time to see that the picture of Mr Michaels *is* gone from Miss Bardwell's desk! I knew it!

It's time to go shopping! I find the supermarket Nora recommended – just round the corner from her flat – it's *sensational*. Once there, I decide to forget the "Mediterranean" theme and just go for a "Sounds really, really tasty" theme instead. I pick a bacon, **leek** and vintage **cheddar puff pastry tart**, some mini **smoked salmon** bagels, some **garlic mushrooms**, ciabatta, and

+++ posh – vornehm +++ to go – zum Mitnehmen +++ obstacle – Hindernis +++ leek – Lauch +++ cheddar = Käsesorte +++ puff pastry tart – Blätterteigpastete +++ smoked salmon – Räucherlachs +++ garlic – Knoblauch +++ mushroom – Champignon +++

something nice to drink. I successfully spend all of the Queen Mother's 50-pound handshake! On one meal!

I don't really have enough money to do the same again for Sam on Saturday now, though. I'll just have to hope there will be some food leftover. *Food leftover from three hungry girls who starve all week at Chalk Farm = not very likely* – but I'll worry about that later.

I **struggle** up the stairs with the shopping and then have a nervous breakdown. Nora has a fridge that looks like she borrowed it from a Playmobil family on a diet. I have to totally **squash** everything to get it to fit. Hmmm. I **bet** you Jamie Oliver doesn't have to work under these conditions.

Anyway, after I've done that, I glance around the flat. Nora's sometimes a bit messy and I'd been a bit worried that the place might still look like it was 1940 and London had just been bombed by my evil German ancestors. Instead, the flat is totally tidy. Everything looks perfect.

It's then that I spot it – an envelope with my name on it, sitting on the telephone table. I go over and look at it more closely: *Emily: Get yourselves a curry PS Don't be scared to use the phone to talk to Germany!* There are 50 pounds inside the envelope. My aunt is always giving me money in envelopes! I love it! My worries about feeding Sam on Saturday are over!

Then I head back to school – arms and head both much lighter.

+++ to struggle – kämpfen +++ to squash – quetschen +++ to bet – wetten +++

What have I done to deserve this?

School's out! I meet Maudie and Kim at Camden **tube** station on Friday evening and we travel the short distance to Fitzrovia together. We're all in a good mood; this is a totally exciting way to be spending Friday night. We have *tonnes* to talk about, of course. We **urgently** need to analyse the Christmas party fiascos. Top of the agenda is what happened with Rob, the guy that Maudie likes a lot – Cyclops flirted with him for half the party. We'll be up till **dawn** talking about it all. The important stuff can wait till we're at Nora's. *In private.* Sitting in the tube, we chat about the holidays first. Kim's were nice though she seems to have spent most of them playing with her **niece** Molly, who's three: "Totally exhausting!"

Maudie's break was *not bad.* She sighs. "6 out of 10. My parents kept giving me career advice. You know the kind of thing: *Have you ever thought about being a* ***lawyer****, darling? Don't you think that would be fascinating?* And when I said no but I *had* thought about becoming a professional DJ, they didn't say *anything* for about a week. It was *great.*"

+++ tube – Londoner U-Bahn +++ urgent – dringend +++ dawn – Sonnenaufgang +++ niece – Nichte +++ lawyer – Anwalt +++

We arrive at Nora's stop. The girls *ooh* and *ahh* at Nora's big neighbour, the BT Tower, right at the end of Cleveland Street. Once we're inside the flat, they're even more impressed. "It's so ***bohemian***," sighs Maudie.

It is. And it's **the real deal**. It's true that Nora's place is packed with what my father would probably call a lot of *Multikulti-Schrott*. But Nora didn't get any of hers at Camden Market. It's all authentic. Everything here has a story: that **rug** in the middle of the floor was a **gift** from a man who wanted to marry her in Morocco. There are some interesting pots from Indonesia that, oh, I can't remember. They were probably from someone else who wanted to marry her. Nora's *hot*.

"Ohhhh!" says Maudie excitedly. "Check out her **vinyl**!" She rushes over to examine Nora's record collection. She sticks something on at once: the Pet Shop Boys! 80's rock – we love it! We're *West End Girls!* I quickly throw the dinner in the **oven**, giving thanks again to the *Gott der Fertiggerichte*. And then we're dancing queens for half an hour, before we become eating queens. Everything tastes amazing. There will be no leftover food, that's clear almost at once. Poor Sam.

I've bought some punch, non-alcoholic, *natürlich* – and it's Maudie who **raises** her glass. "To Emily, for being such an amazing cook! And to Emily's Auntie Nora for letting us come here."

The Pet Shop Boys are still playing in the back-

+++ bohemian – unkonventionell +++ the real deal – der Hammer +++ rug – Teppich +++ gift – Geschenk +++ vinyl – Schallplatte +++ oven – Ofen +++ to raise – erheben +++

ground: it's *What Have I Done to Deserve This?* Which brings us **neatly** to Cyclops and Rob.

Maudie looks **miserable**. "Oh, Amanda's awful. I'm so sorry I didn't believe you, Emily! She's *evil*! So two-faced! She was nice to me when she wanted to get into our party and then …" Maudie falls silent for a moment. She's biting her lip – she's probably wishing it were *Amanda's* lip. "But, well, it seems Rob didn't think she was so bad. He *definitely* took Cyclops' number. I saw him **punching** it **in** to his phone."

Kim sighs. I sigh. Maudie throws her serviette down – yes, I even gave my guests serviettes! I'm good! "Oh, I give up with boys! First Ed, now this. They're all *idiots*."

It's a shame, of course. Rob was the first guy that Maudie had been interested in since Ed. He seemed to be her big chance to move on, get her **confidence** back. Now Cyclops has **torpedoed** that.

"Maybe you didn't make it clear enough to Rob that you like him," I say brightly.

Maudie gives me a look. "Oh, Emily – *get real*. It's totally clear that he's just not that **into me**. He must have a sunglasses fetish."

I smile but it's not actually funny. Not at all. What *is* up with boys, generally? Why do they always like the stupid girls? Even Sam's not totally innocent! He also spent most of the party with Amanda on top of him.

My mind is an open book, it seems, because Kim mutters gently, "What did Sam say about Amanda? I

+++ neat – *hier:* direkt +++ miserable – unglücklich +++ to punch in – eintippen +++ confidence – Vertrauen +++ to torpedo – torpedieren, durchkeuzen +++ to be into s.o. – auf jmdn. stehen +++

watched them after you left and nothing happened but well, he …"

"… didn't *exactly* kick her off," finishes Maudie, darkly. "So what's going on with him?"

And I finally get to tell the girls all about the romantic meeting Sam and me had just before Christmas, about kissing him and both of us saying sorry and kissing him some more. I feel all warm just thinking about us, kissing, with the snow falling around us. I mean, how could that *not* make you feel warm?

Easily, it seems. I mean, Kim smiles but Maudie just rolls her eyes and says things like: *Oh, that's great. Oh, really glad you two* ***sorted it out****. Oh, Sam's sweet.* She doesn't mean any of it, though. She can't. She's had her heart broken again and she's totally anti-boy right now. It will take time before that changes.

The atmosphere in Nora's flat is now about as "**jolly**" as that in a half-empty **funeral parlour**. As hostess, it's my job to try and save the evening. My first act is to switch the Pet Shop Boys off – it's music to kill yourself by. Next, I stick on a DVD I'd rented for the evening. It says on the box that it's *a* ***hilarious*** *romantic comedy*! That will cheer us up!

The film's not too bad and it does take our minds off Rob and Cyclops for a bit, though every time the **lead actor** does anything really nice or kind or loving, Maudie **snorts**. She then complains about the happy

+++ to sort it out – regeln +++ jolly – fröhlich +++ funeral parlour – Aussegnungshalle +++ hilarious – lustig +++ lead actor – Hauptdarsteller +++ to snort – schnauben +++

ending of the film for ages after it's finished. "Real life is nothing like that." Like I said, this is going to take *time.*

The fact that it's tomorrow already helps. Maudie's a bit more cheerful in the morning. She and Kim disappear **pretty** early to get a present for Maudie's mum. "Don't you hate January birthdays?" Maudie **groans**.

I spend the day alone in Nora's flat, tidying up some of the chaos from the night before, doing a bit of home work. I'm just killing time, of course. I'm just waiting for a ring at the downstairs buzzer at 6.30 pm tonight.

I wait. And wait some more. Sam will be **on time**, I'm sure of it.

It's 6.29 pm and I'm watching the **second hand** on Nora's big alarm clock move round and *bzzzzzzzzz!* (or whatever) the buzzer goes downstairs. My heart feels like it's **swallowed** a bird. I can hear footsteps getting closer, closer, closer ...

I open the front door slowly, like someone in a horror movie who's heard a strange noise outside and there he is! I **catch my breath** for a second. Sam looks pale. His hair needs a cut. He's tired. But he's still cuter than cute. He's still my Sam! My Sam!

"My Sam" is still standing in the doorway, **panting.** He's just climbed a serious number of stairs and "my

+++ pretty – *hier:* ziemlich +++ to groan – stöhnen +++ to be on time – pünktlich sein +++ second hand – Sekundenzeiger +++ to swallow – schlucken +++ to catch one's breath – die Luft anhalten +++ to pant – keuchen +++

Sam", like me, is not exactly a sports fanatic. Finally he says, breathlessly, "Where are we?"

I realise that I was so busy being International Girl of Mystery that Sam doesn't even know what on earth he's doing here. I laugh and explain. He smiles and then winks. "Are you going to invite me in for a bottle of **oxygen**?"

At last Sam's officially inside 17 Cleveland Street. He hesitates for a moment and then kisses me. We start kissing in the hall, both of us walking slowly backwards until finally we manage to fall onto Nora's sofa, laughing. We kiss there some more and I'm just lost in Sam again, remembering his smell and how he feels. I don't want to stop but then suddenly Sam does, gasping, "I'm *really* thirsty, Emily!"

"Of course," I mutter quickly. I hurry to the kitchen to get Sam a glass of water. When I come back with it, he's standing next to Nora's over-filled bookshelves. He's enthusiastic: "She's got some great books, your aunt. Have you seen this one about Mark Rothko?" Then he admires some of Nora's photographs that she has hanging on the wall.

It's all a totally cool scene. We could be in a French film or something! And then Sam **spoils** everything. His stomach growls like an angry bear. It's very loud and I can't help but giggle. Sam laughs, too, and looks embarrassed. "Sorry. I'm, like, totally *starving*. Any chance of a sandwich or something?"

"I've got a better idea," I smile. "I'll order us a couple

+++ oxygen – Sauerstoff +++ to spoil – verderben +++

of curries. There's a fantastic restaurant that does take-away around the corner. They have food so **spicy** it'll blow your tongue off. What do you feel like?" I get the takeaway menu from its place of **honour** behind Nora's phone.

Sam pulls a face. "Oh, actually, you know, I'm not *that* hungry. Really, a bit of bread would be fine. A cracker or something." His stomach **rumbles** again. The room shakes.

It's suddenly so obvious. Sam doesn't have any money. And we've had this before: the date we had in Regent's Park last year, it was the same then. Sam suddenly *wasn't really hungry.* He suddenly felt like *having the smallest thing on the menu.* And his phone – not working, eh? Hmmm. I'm starting to wonder.

I don't say anything. I just pick up the envelope that Nora left for us and show it to Sam silently. He **peers** inside and then looks totally shocked. Finally he mumbles, "Your aunt: *respect.* Oh, go on then. I'll have a chicken madras. And some mushroom pakora. Oh, and can we have a bit of nan bread, too? Couple of popadoms?"

Not hungry, eh?

I order the food and we sit on the sofa and wait. Sam holds my hand, then **strokes** my face. He looks at me a bit shyly and says, "Emily, thanks for your Christmas presents. The DVD and the picture you gave me for

+++ spicy – scharf +++ honour – Ehre +++ to rumble – *hier:* knurren +++ to peer – spähen +++ to stroke – streicheln +++

Christmas. Me and Mrs White. **Cosmic**. Honestly, I love it."

I gave Sam a photo I took of him sitting in White Out, our favourite café, centre of our Camden universe, where they do London's best chips. Hmmm, I'm starving, too, actually. I wonder where our food is?

Our curries finally arrive. We eat and make a bit of polite conversation about photography again. Sam's finished in no time; I eat more slowly. I'm nervous. I have the feeling that the *important thing* Sam has to tell me is connected with money, somehow, or his family perhaps, but what if I'm wrong? I'm not getting "break-up **vibes**", but then I didn't get them when Ed Stanton finished with me **either**.

When I have finally finished eating, Sam opens his mouth to speak. He takes a deep breath. I close my eyes, just for a second. Then it all comes out.

+++ cosmic – *hier:* genial +++ vibe – Schwingung +++ not ... either – auch nicht +++

Stand by My Man?

Sam starts by telling me what I already know: he has two very different lives, one in Scotland, and one here in London. "My parents aren't rich. We're really normal, I **suppose**, **apart from** the fact that Dad doesn't live with us. But I suppose that *is* normal."

Sam's mum works in an **insurance** office and his dad works for a telecoms company. Or at least he *did* work for one. Sam plays nervously with the silver **foil dish** that his curry came in. "Dad's got diabetes and he's been very ill **recently**. I didn't tell you – he had to give up his job in October."

He lost his job in *October*. Sam and me started going out together in November and Sam didn't say a word to me. I never asked much about his family either, of course. My **fault**, too.

Sam **crushes** the curry dish suddenly with his hand. "Christmas was a nightmare. My dad's a bit of a **mess** and he can't give us any money. Nothing."

He throws the silver ball that he's made out of the

+++ to suppose – vermuten +++ apart from – abgesehen von +++ insurance – Versicherung +++ foil – Folie +++ dish – *hier:* Schale +++ recently – in letzter Zeit +++ fault – Fehler +++ to crush – zerknüllen +++ to be a mess – unordentlich sein +++

dish across the room. "We thought at first that Dad would get a new job easily, but it hasn't happened that way. He's just too ill. I don't know when he'll be able to work again or *if* he'll be able to work again."

Sam stares at me. "My phone wasn't broken. My mum didn't have the money for the **bill**. I've got a **pay-as-you-go** one now. I'm going to sell my laptop and that will give me some spending money for a bit. But it's so expensive here – sometimes it feels like *breathing* costs money in London."

I'm very, very *slow* to pick up on things, sometimes, have you noticed? It's only now that I really understand what Sam is trying to tell me.

"I can't **stand it** any more," he says, quietly. "Being so far away when things are this hard at home. I had a long talk with my parents at Christmas. There's no way they can keep paying for St Dougan's – they never really *could* **afford** it. So it's all decided. I'm going to go back to school in Scotland at the end of the school year."

Sam's the oldest of three brothers. He's calm, quiet and kind and the **rock** of his family, I have the feeling. They need him. I understand that. *But I need him, too!*

I want to **reach out** to him now. I want to be Sam's rock. But all I feel is panic. I don't want Sam to leave London. But I don't want to cry and be hysterical either. I just sit there on Nora's blue sofa, with a stupid frozen face, like I've eaten a kilogramme of Botox. I'm so sad

+++ bill – Rechnung +++ pay-as-you-go – pre-paid +++ to stand it – es aushalten +++ to afford – sich leisten +++ rock – Fels +++ to reach out to s.o. – *hier:* jmdn. berühren +++

for Sam but I can't *show* him that. I'm too scared. So I don't do *anything*. I'm about as useful to Sam as a chocolate **teapot**. You know, *wie ein Skilift in Ostfriesland, ein Herrenklo im Nonnenkloster, ein Kühlschrank für Eskimos etc.* You get the picture.

Sam's smiling now, bravely. "It's not the end of the world, you know. Being here with all these rich kids – it drives me crazy sometimes. I'd like to be at a normal school again, really." He pauses for a moment, just a second too long. "It's a shame about the band, of course. But they'll soon find another drummer."

"The band!" I cry and put my hand over my mouth. Like a real drama queen – Sam looks annoyed. "I can't ask my parents to **bankrupt themselves** so I can stay on here and play drums. And we do have rock bands in Scotland, too, you know."

Sam **clears his throat**. He's finished explaining things at home to me and he's now going to tell me what all this means for us – I can *feel it*.

Sam's staring at a large statue of an African **warrior** that Nora has standing next to her TV. The warrior is nearly twice the size of the TV set and has a giant **spear** in its hand. Nora got the statue in Botswana, I think, and right now, it seems to be threatening us: *Sort this out or I'll kill you!*

Sam senses the threat, too. Looking a bit nervously at the warrior's spear, Sam says, "I'm just not sure if the

+++ teapot – Teekanne +++ to bankrupt oneself – sich verschulden +++ to clear one's throat – sich räuspern +++ warrior – Krieger +++ spear – Speer +++

two of us is such a good idea, Emily. I've been a terrible boyfriend, let's **face** it. And we've got exams coming up, I want to do some stuff with the band before I go. Play another couple of **gigs**. Perhaps it's better if the two of us don't get too close."

Maybe I'm imagining it but it seems as though when Sam says the words *too close*, he moves just 5.8 centimetres or so away from me. "We'll only have to say goodbye in a few months anyway. You'll go back to Berlin then, too. Is it **worth it**?"

It might seem, written down on paper, in black and white, that Sam's asking what clever people call a *rhetorical question* – a question that's not really a question. A question you know the answer to already. But, as he says it to me, I don't have the feeling that Sam's already decided to finish things with me. I have the feeling that he doesn't know what to do.

He's blushing now. "This will sound totally **slimy** but you're a really pretty girl, Emily. Maybe you should just enjoy your freedom in London."

I'm still expressionless. I'm staring at the statue of the warrior now, wondering **vaguely** what kind of wood it's made of. And I'm remembering something that Kim once said to me, after I hunted Ed Stanton down in a supermarket. She called me a *warrior princess*. Now it's time to be brave again. Part of me feels like crying and ***begging*** Sam not to finish with me. Another part of me knows that's a *disaster* of an idea.

+++ to face sth. – einer Sache ins Auge sehen +++ gig – Auftritt +++ to be worth it – es wert sein +++ slimy – schleimig +++ vague – vage, undeutlich +++ to beg s.o. – jmdn. anflehen +++

So, instead, I say in a business-like tone: "Shall we both take some time out to think about things?" *Time out.* I sound like I'm 50 and on my third divorce.

Sam nods, very slowly. "Time out," he repeats. "Yeah, that's a good plan." He stares at me for a moment. It's painful. He's so near and yet so far. Soon, he'll tell me that he has to go back to school. And I don't want him to. Sam turns his head: "I suppose I'd better make a move. Got to be back at Guantanamo by ten or they'll call the cops."

We sit for just a moment longer at our opposite ends of the sofa. And then Sam says softly, "Are we allowed just one more kiss?" and I think for about 0.0000998 seconds before I say, *Yessssss!* and I jump at him.

Sam finally heads back to school, leaving me alone in Nora's flat. It's only *9.30 pm.*

Remember I said how *great* it was to be by myself? How *great* it was to have some privacy? Well, that was then and this is now and now, **all of a sudden**, it doesn't seem that *great*. I suddenly feel like I'll go crazy here by myself! *Help!* The walls will close in on me! I'll start hearing voices! I'm hearing them now: Nora's phone seems to be whispering to me *Call Berlin! Call Berlin!*

Well, Nora did specifically say it was OK to use the phone to call Germany, didn't she? I mean, she *probably* meant ringing my parents, but I haven't talked to my best friends Betti and Merle for ages. I hate phoning them from school. Just a quick half/three quarters of an hour, lying on the sofa and knowing no one can hear me. And it's *sort of* an emergency call. The situation with Sam is a *real* crisis, after all. Betti *is* my love guru: she'll know exactly what to do.

I call my parents first – no answer! Brilliant! I leave a quick message on the *AB* saying that I'm fine, *blah, blah* and then I ring Betti's place – 0800 LIEBESGURU. I've already checked by text where Betti and Merle would be.

How long did I say the conversation would last? Three quarters of an hour? That was a bit conservative, I must say. It's a boy talk marathon with Merle and Betti. I tell them all about my brand new crisis/dilemma with Sam. I can't tell you everything that was said in response in the next two hours so I'll summarise:

Emily Hausmann soll mit Sam Reid Schluss machen – eine Stimme.

+++ all of a sudden – plötzlich +++

Emily Hausmann soll für die Liebe mit Sam Reid kämpfen – eine Stimme.
Stimmenthaltung – eine.

Weitere Punkte: M und B sind dabei, Flüge nach London zu buchen – Termin im April vorgeschlagen (Osterferien Germany). EH stimmte zu.

Gespräch offiziell beendet.

Hmmm, not very helpful, **on the whole**. I could have guessed all that before. Betti, the *ewige Pragmatikerin*, voted to finish with Sam, of course. "Du kennst doch das Buch *He's just not that into you?* Schatz. Haben wir zusammen gelesen. Ich sag es dir jetzt sehr deutlich – Sam's just not that into you, baby."

Merle, of course, is the *ewige Romantikerin*. "Emily, Liebe ist alles, was wir haben. Nichts ist heiliger, wichtiger. Du kannst nicht einfach so aufgeben. Sam leidet momentan – du musst ihn doch unterstützen!"

Me? I'm somewhere in the middle: an *ewige Pragmantikerin*, perhaps? I can understand what Betti's thinking. On the other hand, I can see Merle's **point of view** totally. I really do have the feeling that Sam was thinking about what was best for me. I think he likes me enough to want me to be happy.

And shouldn't this be the time to stand by my man? Instead of walking away because his life is complicated/poor/boring? Is that really a nice thing to do?

+++ on the whole – alles in allem +++ point of view – Standpunkt +++

I wake up with the feeling on Sunday morning that I need to **reboot**, do something else. I want to take some photos – that's my favourite way to relax. Even if I only make it to the BT tower and back that will do.

It takes me ages to get ready to go out, somehow. I'm tired and everything I do today seems to be in hyper **slow motion**. It doesn't help that Nora's phone keeps ringing. The answering machine is on, of course, but I still jump every time it goes.

I can't help but listen to the messages that are left, too. A lot of calls seem to be about work – even though it's Sunday morning. One **editor** phones three times: he's desperate to get Nora to photograph quite a famous actress tomorrow. I feel like picking up the phone and saying, "I'll do it!"

I'm finally getting my shoes on when the phone rings again. I've got so used to people leaving messages that I've almost stopped listening. Almost. Then it strikes me – there is something *very **familiar*** about that voice. *Have you been good girls?* It's Santa! I mean, Mr Michaels!

He doesn't sound all jolly and Santa-like now. He sounds quite desperate: *Nora, if you're there, please pick up. I don't even know where you are. I keep calling your mobile but it's always switched off. Are you all right? I wanted to tell you that I've finished things with Connie. I need to talk to you …*

This really is Far Too Much Information. Too per-

+++ to reboot – neu starten +++ slow motion – Zeitlupe +++ editor – Redakteur/in +++ familiar – bekannt +++

sonal! Spontaneously, I rush over and pick up the phone.

It's terrible: when I answer, just for a moment, Mr Michaels obviously thinks it's Nora on the line. "Finally!" he says, sounding ecstatic. "I was getting worried."

Stop! Don't talk! Breathlessly, at high speed, I say, "Sir, it's me, Emily, Sir, Nora's niece, I'm staying at Nora's flat for the weekend, Sir, but she's not here. She's in Beirut. Sir."

I'm not quite sure why I keep saying "Sir" to Mr Michaels. That's what we call our **male** teachers here, of course – it's all "Sir" this and "Miss" that for the ladies – but still, it's a bit strange to be doing this on the phone, at the weekend, in Nora's flat. It must be a nervous tic. It's also a stupid tic.

There's a long silence at the other end of the phone. **I can't wait for** Mr Michaels to speak so that we can finish this conversation. I'm bright red, actually. Mr Michaels finally coughs, "Ah yes, Emily, of course. Beirut. I must have forgotten."

Right, Sir. Sure. Like you "forget" someone saying they were going to *Beirut.* It's not as if Nora said she was *just going to Aldi for a* ***loaf of bread*** or anything. Nora didn't tell him where she was off to, it's clear.

Then Mr Michaels asks, in a *sort-of-oh-so-casual-I-don't-really-care-oh-yes-I-do-really* kind of voice, "I can't remember when she said she'd be coming back. Do you know?"

+++ male – männlich +++ I can't wait for – *hier:* ich kann es kaum erwarten, dass … +++ loaf of bread – Laib Brot +++

I tell him that Nora said something about three or four weeks. I make it sound vague because it probably is. Mr Michaels mutters again, "Oh yes, yes, yes, now I remember." There's another *really* long pause before he says again, "Are you well, Emily?" And I say yes and then we can both hang up on each other, **relieved**.

It's **confirmed** – *I've finished things with Connie.* He must have done it for Nora. Pray for me.

+++ relieved – erleichtert +++ to confirm – bestätigen +++

Back from Bangkok

Keep busy. Some photo therapy. At last, I get out of the flat with my camera. I take pictures of the BT Tower and some interesting buildings in the area around it. There's lots to shoot here – some nice **Georgian** architecture at Fitzroy **Square**, for instance. I use up four rolls of film and I feel much better about everything when I'm finished.

It's around six o'clock when I'm finally back at school. I don't feel great about what happened with Sam but I feel a bit more **refreshed** after my mini photo shoot. Refreshed until I open the door to the dorm, **that is**. A strange, very *un*refreshing smell hits me straight away. It's, oh, what is it? A *Räucherstäbchen.* **Incense.** Jasmine. The **scent** of the east. Guess who's back from Bangkok?

Cyclops is standing right in front of me now, hands on her **bony hips**. She's wearing a **tight** white T-shirt – *It's January! It's London! Hello!* – and tight white jeans. This is an outfit specially chosen to **show off** the fact that

+++ Georgian – georgianischer Stil (1720–1840) +++ square – Platz +++ refreshed – erfrischt +++ that is – zumindest +++ incense – Rauch von Räucherstäbchen +++ scent – Duft +++ bony – knochig +++ hip – Hüfte +++ tight – eng +++ to show sth. off – mit etw. protzen +++

Amanda is no longer that pale, unhealthy colour that most British people (including me) seem to be. She's now a very dark cocoa-brown colour. She's sweated over that **tan**. That's probably why she was a week late. Missed her flight – ha! I don't think Amanda *ever* planned to come back on time.

Amanda has a pair of sunglasses pushed back over her hair, which is also blonder. She obviously thinks she looks amazing. Unfortunately, she sort of does.

I haven't moved from the **doorway**. Cyclops and me are still staring at each other. *Faceoff*. The last time I saw her she was staring at me from Sam's knee, of course. Neither of us has forgotten that. I was stupidly nervous of Cyclops before but it's a new year. The **gloves are coming off**. Oh, yes.

+++ tan – Sonnenbräune +++ doorway – Türöffnung +++ The gloves are coming off – Jetzt werden härtere Geschütze aufgefahren +++

Cyclops is just grinning at me: "Oh, Emily, darling, are you sick? You look awful. You're as white as a ghost." She throws herself down on her bed and stretches out, like some kind of evil, suntanned pussycat. "I'm guessing you haven't seen Sam for a while? He would certainly put some colour in your **cheeks**. We had an absolutely *amazing* time at the party. Oh, on holiday sometimes, I couldn't sleep. Impossible to decide: Sam or Rob? Rob or Sam?"

Miaaaoowwww. It's more than time to show my claws. "Nice tan, Cyclops," I say easily. "So bad for your skin, of course. You'll look like Keith Richards in a couple of years. Does the school nurse check for **melanoma**?"

It's the first time I have ever called her *Cyclops* to her face. And Keith Richards – it's a declaration of war, no more, no less.

Amanda plainly can't believe it. "**How dare you?**" She's speaking very slowly, very clearly. "How dare you call me that? I'll tell Miss Bardwell first thing tomorrow!"

Here's where Amanda finds out the real cost of her all over tan. She's missed the action all over Chalk Farm while she was creaming herself with cocoa butter in Phuket. Information is power here. And Amanda is suddenly totally powerless.

I throw myself down on my bed, too – we're now lying facing each other. "Oh, I think you'll find that Miss

+++ cheek – Wange +++ melanoma – Hautkrebs +++
How dare you? – Wie kannst du es wagen? +++

Bardwell won't be interested. She has problems of her own."

I have to be careful here. I shouldn't have heard what Mr Michaels said on Nora's answering machine. But it's clear to everyone that Mr Michaels and Miss Bardwell have split up. So let Amanda learn about it from someone else. Let her sweat.

Cyclops isn't sweating yet. She is looking at me blankly. She has absolutely no idea what I'm talking about.

I'll just be **enigmatic** – that will *kill* her. "Oh, you'll find out soon enough," I laugh. "You've missed a few things, put it that way. And I did see Sam yesterday **by the way**. We were talking about you, funnily enough. What was it Sam called you again? Oh, I remember – a total *nightmare*."

Amanda's tan turns one **shade** lighter – sort of latte macchiato instead of espresso. "You're lying, you stupid ***Kraut***," she **hisses**. "Anyway, Rob is the one for me. Your little Scotsman is too boring."

Wow, things got nasty pretty quickly, didn't they? The gloves are not just off – they've been thrown right out of the window, onto the hockey pitch. And how should I respond to being called a Kraut?? *Nein, ich lüge nicht, Tommy.* I feel like we're standing in a **battlefield** in Normandy, suddenly.

"Half-Kraut, thanks," I say calmly. "And you haven't got a chance with Rob. I'll bet you anything …"

+++ enigmatic – rätselhaft +++ by the way – übrigens +++ shade – Schattierung +++ Kraut – Schimpfwort für Deutsche +++ to hiss – zischen +++ battlefield – Schlachtfeld +++

Wetten, dass ...

It was a stupid thing to say, I **admit** it. I know it as soon as the stupid words have left my stupid mouth. Amanda's face brightens: "You'll bet me *anything*? Is that what you just said??"

"Well, emmm," I mumble, suddenly uncertain.

I didn't mean it, of course. I don't know Rob at all. Maudie *did* say he seemed interested in Amanda. He took her phone number. It seems a bit of a high-risk **gamble**, now I think about it. Not really my style.

"I bet you I *can* get a date with Rob Carpenter ..." – she knows his surname, bad sign! – "... this week! Come on then, what are the **stakes**? Not money, of course, I mean it's clear – you don't have *any*."

Amanda gives my baggy old grey *H&M* **cardigan** – Saison 2003! – a look that has a *ph-Wert* of about one. I've made a mistake, I know it. Cyclops probably can get a date with Rob, but she won't be able to keep him, **no way**. I can't let her win, I *can't*.

"OK," I sigh, "the bet is this: if by some miracle you

+++ to admit – zugeben +++ gamble – Glücksspiel +++ stakes – Einsatz +++ cardigan – Strickjacke +++ no way – auf keinen Fall +++

stay with Rob Carpenter for longer than eight weeks, then you get my …"

I look around the room desperately. The first thing I see is my camera, which I always have next to my bed. There's no way I'm betting that, of course. But there's a **glint** in Amanda's eye now. She saw me glance at my camera, I sense it, and she knows what it means to me.

My mind is racing. *What else can I offer her? A* ***kidney****? My little brother Max?* "My iPod," I say quickly.

Amanda just laughs. "Your iPod's older than me, darling. I suppose it *might* be **valuable**. A prototype, was it?" She's playing with me now. "I think you can do better. What about … your *camera*, for instance? It's not even *digital*. It's worthless, right? You wouldn't care about losing an old thing like that." And she actually goes over to my camera and *strokes it*.

I would rather bite my own legs off than lose my camera, as Amanda knows only too well. I'm thinking, thinking, thinking. Eight weeks is *ages*. If Maudie likes Rob, he must be a good guy. He'll see through Amanda straight away. I must have **faith** in human nature.

"Fine," I say, trying to sound **confident**. *Fine*. I'm certain I can hear my camera **whimpering** like a **puppy** that's just been kicked. I try to ignore it.

Amanda smiles and sits up. "Your camera it is. My last **relationship** lasted eight months, you might like to know. Eight weeks is *nothing*."

+++ glint – Glitzern +++ kidney – Niere +++ valuable – wertvoll +++ faith – Glaube, Vertrauen +++ confident – *hier:* zuversichtlich +++ to whimper – wimmern +++ puppy – Welpe +++ relationship – Beziehung +++

Eight months? What have I done???? I'm probably going to lose my most **treasured** possession and Maudie will **go nuts** if she finds out that I've **challenged** Cyclops to get a date with Rob! I'm pushing her into Rob's arms. I'm a **traitor**.

Luckily for me right now, Cyclops seems to have other worries, too. She needs to see Miss Bardwell, I can *smell* it. She mutters something about going to find her "best friends" Laurie and the twins, but I'm certain she's off to find Miss Bardwell. *Certain.*

I'm alone again with my camera. It must hate me. I look at it guiltily. I feel like a mother who's just offered to sell her child or something. I'm a monster. *Inhuman.*

We had better make the most of the time we have left together. I take the films from my photo shoot this

+++ treasured – liebevoll gehütet +++ to go nuts – durchdrehen +++ to challenge – herausfordern +++ traitor – Verräter/in +++ we had better – wir sollten besser +++

morning and head off to the darkroom and develop them. They're disappointing, really. Quite a lot are **shaky** and badly framed. Some of the ones of the BT Tower are cool, though. It's such a space age, retro building, I love it. I'll stick the **decent** ones in my photo diary straight away.

Nora gave me my photo diary when I arrived here and I've done my best to keep it **up to date**. It will be a brilliant momento of my crazy year here in London …

I've only managed to stick in two photos when Melissa and Becks return from jogging together round the **running track**, it seems. They're ***nutters***: it's so dark and cold outside now. But it's been worth it. The girls have got news. Breathless, sweaty news: "Emily, it's really true! It's over – Miss Bardwell and Mr Michaels!"

While they were running 680 times round the track in the darkness, it seems that Melissa and Becks met Catherine – *Catherine Taggart, you know? Fourth form? Oh Emily, you don't know anyone!*

Melissa is wiping her **forehead** with a pink towel: "Catherine Taggart's mother's friend's cousin is Miss Bardwell's best friend. Miss Bardwell visited her on Saturday and told her that she's split up with Mr Michaels. She said that they'd just grown apart but no one believes that and …"

She stops suddenly and eyes me carefully. "But you knew all this already anyway, didn't you?"

It's true. I should have looked more surprised at this

+++ shaky – zittrig, verwackelt +++ decent – ganz gut, anständig +++ up to date – auf dem neuesten Stand +++ running track – Laufstrecke +++ nutter – Verrückte/r +++ forehead – Stirn +++

news, probably. "Hmmm?" I say casually. I carry on sticking my photos in my album. My hands are a bit shaky suddenly.

"Emily," says Melissa, in a serious voice, red face **leaning** towards me. "Did you know that they'd split up?"

Becks, who is still running on the spot for some reason, shouts, "Did he leave Miss B for Nora?"

They call a *Notlüge* a *white lie* in English. Right now, I decide that there's enough *Not* to whitewash things a bit. I look up calmly at the two glowing faces, staring at me questioningly. "No," I say, "I didn't know. But we'd all guessed, right? Nora's in Beirut. I haven't talked to her. She's totally *not* into Mr Michaels though. No way."

Becks and Melissa look at me **suspiciously**. Finally Becks says, "OK. I'll go first in the shower, Mel. You always take *hours* ..." and I can breathe again. I'm **off the hook**. For the moment.

Melissa picks up a magazine – *Horse and Hound*, her favourite one – and **flicks** through it. She's really watching me, I have a feeling. I am actually more interesting to Melissa right now than **a bunch of** old horse pictures! I'm hot!

I **carry on** sticking pictures in my album. Neither Melissa nor me speak. Everything is quiet, except for the sound of Becks singing loudly and **tunelessly** in the shower. Things stay like this until about 15 minutes later when Amanda blows in and announces loud and proud

+++ to lean – (sich) lehnen +++ suspicious – misstrauisch +++ to be off the hook – aus dem Schneider sein +++ to flick – *hier:* blättern +++ a bunch of – ein Haufen +++ to carry on – weitermachen +++ tuneless – falsch +++

that *she's got a date with Rob Carpenter on Friday night.* She can show me his text message if I want **proof**. (I *soooo* don't.) They'll be "dining" at Bijous, a charming little French restaurant that Amanda's father recommended.

Cyclops looks absolutely triumphant: "I love that place, so expensive, but they do heavenly *Boeuf Bourguignon*."

In the background we can hear Becks singing: *I was made for loving you, baby* in the shower. I really, really hope that Rob wasn't made for loving Amanda.

Amanda grunts. "She sings like she **snores**, that girl." Then she flicks a switch hidden somewhere on her body to "charming" and smiles, "Oh, and Melissa, any idea what's up with Miss Bardwell? I just saw her and, well, she seemed a bit odd. She wouldn't …"

Wouldn't talk to me. I'm sure that's what she had been about to say. Ha! Amanda obviously couldn't get any information out of her brain-dead **entourage** either. She must be desperate if she's asking Melissa for gossip in front of me.

Melissa just shrugs, looking uncertain. "Oh, emmm, I don't know. She has seemed a bit **down in the dumps**, **lately**, it's true." She turns over another page in her horse magazine, nervously.

Amanda eyes me suspiciously. "This wouldn't have anything to do with your crazy aunt, would it, Hausmann? Because I'm warning you – *it had better not.*"

+++ proof – Beweis +++ to snore – schnarchen +++ entourage (frz.) – Gefolge +++ down in the dumps – niedergeschlagen +++ lately – in letzter Zeit +++

Then Cyclops smiles at me, a real 600 megawatt **blast** of evil in my face, "Does eight weeks with Rob count from now or from Friday, mon petit fromage?"

My little cheese??? Is that what she just called me? I'm pretty useless at French, actually. You could write all the French words I know on the back of a very small envelope – envelope, camembert, baguette, brie, déjà vu. You know – *that totally weird feeling you have when you suddenly feel like you've been here before.* And déjà vu is *exactly* what I experience on Wednesday.

I'm *chez moi* (OK, one more) in dorm 3B, enjoying a quiet moment. I'm actually trying to stick all the photos I didn't finish putting into my album on Sunday, when Amanda comes in and spoils things. Quiet moments never last at Chalk Farm School – I'm on my second picture *again* when there's a knock at the door. Before I can say anything, Kim – a very sweaty Kim – **bursts into** the room.

I'm surprised to see her. Kim has never been in the magical world of dorm 3B before. The dorm is so small and so full of Cyclops that we never normally meet here. It must be urgent.

Kim's just been jogging, by the look of her. She has on a nice green **towelling tracksuit**. She's a bit breathless – she must have run up all our stairs, too. It *is* urgent, it seems.

"I had to come now," she gasps. "Have you heard?"

+++ blast – Druckwelle +++ to burst into – hineinplatzen in +++ towelling – Frottee- +++ tracksuit – Jogginganzug +++

While Kim was running – the track is obviously *the* Chalk Farm gossip factory – she met Trudie Derby – *you must know Trudie? Fifth form? Oh Emily, don't you know anyone?*

Anyway, Trudie's cousin's dog's boyfriend's cleaner's flatmate (oh, something like that!) is friends with Amanda Dobson's mum, "and she told *her* that Amanda's got a date with a lovely boy called Rob! It *must* be Maudie's Rob, don't you …"

Kim has a pink towel with her and wipes at her forehead. (It's only actually at this point that I think: *I have been here before.*) Then she stops suddenly and **tilts** her head to one side. "But you knew all this already anyway, didn't you?"

It's true. I should have looked more surprised at this news, probably. "Hmmm," I mutter, casually. I carry on sticking my photos in my album. My hands are a bit shaky suddenly.

"Emily," says Kim, in a serious voice. "*Did* you know?"

I look up and try to act surprised. "No," I mumble, "I didn't know."

Kim looks at me suspiciously. Then, finally, it seems she's satisfied. "OK, but I don't want Maudie to hear this from anyone else. One of us has to tell her. Should it be me or you?"

"It's probably better if you tell her," I say, very quietly. "I mean, you're closer to her …"

Kim is still a bit suspicious: she obviously thinks what I've just said – *you're closer to Maudie* – is strange.

+++ to tilt – drehen +++

There's always been a *tiny* bit of **rivalry** between Kim and me about who's "closer" to Maudie.

"Right, well, yes, I'll tell her then," she says slowly. She's now rubbing her hair with her towel. We make a loose date to meet in a couple of days and Kim shuts the door.

As she shuts the door, I shut my photo album. Then I hit myself in the face with it and repeat to myself 600 times the words: *I am a big stupid idiot.*

What am I doing? What have I done? Not only did I make a stupid bet on Maudie's love life, I've just lied to Kim about doing it. I'll have to tell both girls what I've done, of course. But not tonight. Soon. Really soon, honest.

+++ rivalry – Rivalität +++

Mein Sebastian???

Right now, I have to keep a clear head. Dates – I've got it in my diary. Amanda had her first meeting with Rob on the 16th of January. I go forward eight weeks. They have to stay together until March the 13th. They can't possibly do it. No way. I mean, how could anyone **bear** to go out with Amanda for longer than 20 seconds? She's a good actress but surely even she can't act *all the time.*

No, I decide confidently – the relationship will be long over before the Easter holidays. I'll be able to laugh about my bet with Betti and Merle when they visit me then. The English and the German Easter holidays **overlap** for a week, thankfully, and the plan is that we should stay at Nora's together then. I wonder if my Berlin "**homies**" have booked their flights yet. Time to do a bit of Facebook, German style, and see.

I head off to a computer room and I log in. There it is – official. Betti and Merle HAVE booked their flights to London! HURRAH! *April 6 – 13th*. OK, great. I'm just about to log out again when I notice it … Sebastian Junger has sent me a **hug**!

+++ to bear – (er)tragen +++ to overlap – überlappen +++ homie – Kumpel +++ hug – Umarmung +++

I can't believe it! After months of silence, here he is. Sebastian Junger, remember him? You probably don't. *I* nearly don't. I was in love with him for years back at Hermann-Hesse but – the **fool**! – he ignored me for Katharina Müller, our in-house *Superzicke* and *damals* my *allerliebste Erzfeindin*. Betti and Merle have been saying things like: *Sebastian wollte dich anrufen/eine Mail schicken* for months, but I've heard nothing.

And now here he is. There's not just a hug, there's a message:

Emily! Wollte dir – ein bisschen verspätet vielleicht – nur ein frohes Neues wünschen! Wie geht es dir in der Stadt der Städte? Ist London tatsächlich cooler als Berlin? Hier ist es eigentlich stinklangweilig. Habe von Betti und Merle gehört, dass sie dich zu Ostern besuchen kommen. Bin neidisch – soll ich dich vielleicht auch mal besuchen? Eigentlich vermisse ich dich sehr. Aber wahrscheinlich wird dann dein neuer Freund stinksauer, oder? Stimmt es wirklich, dass er Schotte ist? Trägt er einen Schottenrock? Spielt er Dudelsack??? Sag Bescheid. War noch nie in London. Dein Sebastian.

Mein Sebastian? Really? After all this time and with all these miles/kilometres between us, he's suddenly mine?? And all I can think is: *nicht jetzt.*

Oh, I wish Sebastian hadn't **got in touch**, I really do. It's ***confusing***.

+++ fool – Idiot +++ to get in touch – sich melden +++ confusing – verwirrend +++

But I certainly wish that Sam *would* get in touch with me. He won't – it's my move. I have to decide whether we have a future or not. I still haven't **made up my mind**. Bad songs and/or stupid people always tell you to *listen to your heart* at times like these. My heart, it seems, has no idea what to do. It's keeping its hearty mouth shut.

My brain, on the other hand, is trying. It's being quite logical. *Logically* speaking, it's not like Sam and me dated forever. It wasn't even six weeks. So although I thought I might be in love with him, shouldn't it be possible just to "love" him as a friend? Stop laughing. I'm only 14, but I've seen *Harry und Sally*. It can't happen. You can't be friends with someone you find attractive, right? It's **doomed**.

Where is Betti's *Top-Liebestest* when you need it? I try to "test" the boys I was "friends" with in Berlin. Sebastian, of course: bad start. We were – are – "friends" but it was always pretty clear that I **had a crush on** him. And now he seems a tiny bit interested in me. The world's gone *mad*.

I try to think of other examples from life at Hermann-Hesse. Merle was once "nur befreundet" with a boy in the year below us, but that turned sour. Don't ask. Betti was quite friendly with Lars-Christoph Schmid, but then he started sending her **creepy** *Herr der Ringe* love letters and stalking her … or something. I must ask her what's going on there. She's stopped talking about him.

+++ to make up one's mind – sich entscheiden +++ doomed – dem Untergang geweiht +++ to have a crush on s.o. – in jmdn. verknallt sein +++ creepy – gruselig +++

I'm just about to give up when – **Eureka!** – I think of it. Nora! Nora has *hundreds* of male friends, other journalists and photographers mainly. She can do it. It *must* be possible. I can't stand the thought of losing Sam completely, but he's right – it's the wrong time to try to be together. We will be the first couple ever who fancy each other to just be friends. They will name streets after us.

I've done it. I've made up my mind. I call Sam right away and ask to meet tonight. He's surprised: it's already 6.30 pm and he's just started writing a history essay. "It's important," I say meaningfully. This is plainly a code for: *I've decided what we should do*, so he quickly replies, "White Out at 7.00?"

Suits me. Even though we could theoretically still go to Nora's flat, I don't want to. It will be too rushed to get back for **curfew** and it seems too *intimate*, the two of us alone, sitting on Nora's sofa, knees touching. Too much **temptation**. And I haven't eaten proper chips since *before Christmas*. I'm getting all shaky, like I'm **going cold turkey** or something. I need a hit of chips.

The race is on. I must get to White Out before Sam. It was one of my New Year's **resolutions** not to be late all the time. I throw the first warm thing I can find over my school uniform and rush out of the door. I'm also driven by my need for chips. I can almost *smell* them.

I'm there! It's not even seven yet and there's no sign of Sam, hurrah! I peer through White Out's big glass

+++ Eureka! – Juhuu! +++ to suit – passen +++ curfew – Ausgangssperre +++ temptation – Versuchung +++ to go cold turkey – auf Entzug sein +++ resolution – Neujahrsvorsatz +++

window, praying that I won't **spot** him sitting there as usual, waiting patiently for me. I don't. Instead, I see something really horrific. If you're **squeamish**, look away now:

It could be worse, I suppose. It could be Ed Stanton and Miss Bardwell sitting there, gazing into each others' eyes, for instance. It's still pretty bad – it's Cyclops and Rob doing the gazing instead.

+++ to spot – entdecken +++ squeamish – zimperlich +++

In the Friends Zone

Oh, **for goodness sake**! What on earth are *they* doing here? Amanda's posh! She eats things like canapés and Boeuf Bourguignon – not chips. She doesn't belong here. She probably just wants to see how the other half live or something. I've heard her call White Out "White **Trash**" before. **The nerve**.

She looks pretty *white trashy* herself right now, Cyclops. She's not wearing a **fur** coat and diamonds – not quite. She *is* wearing a very tight sapphire blue dress, over which she has "thrown" the **pashmina** that she got from Santa/Miss Bardwell at the Christmas party. She's holding Rob's hand across the table. Rob is talking and Amanda is looking at him as though he's explaining the meaning of life and the universe to her.

Everything about the picture in front of me is wrong. They really are a totally odd couple – it's like Verona Pooth going out with Pete Doherty. Rob is cute, no question, but he looks very rough and very white. His hair could do with a good brush. He's still wearing his uniform, which obviously has a label inside which says

+++ For goodness sake! – Herrgott nochmal! +++ trash – Müll, Kitsch +++ The nerve – Die hat Nerven +++ fur – Pelz +++ pashmina – Kaschmirschal +++

"Do not **iron**". Amanda, on the other hand, looks as though she has a GSG9-style team of personal stylists on 24-hour standby.

I'm still standing frozen outside the window of White Out. I definitely can't see Sam, so it looks like I have actually managed to get here first. That's good. It means we won't have to go inside and talk to Amanda. Sam hates her now.

I watch Amanda and Rob a little bit more, through the window, carefully trying to stay out of sight. I can't help it. I stare at them the way you would at a car crash. Except this is a much bigger disaster. It's more like the Space Shuttle has made an emergency landing on Chalk Farm Road.

Amanda is now actually clicking her fingers in the air and shouting "Waiter!" at *Mrs White*. It's the first time I've ever seen Mrs White look unfriendly! No wonder: Amanda seems to want to discuss every **item** on the menu. I can just imagine the conversation:

Amanda: Do you have **low-fat** dressing on your Caesar salad? Or anything with no **carbs**?

Mrs White: We don't have low-fat anything, dearie. We have chips, chips and chips. All with lots of fat.

It's a funny scene but I'm still worried. Amanda and Rob's date at the **fancy** French restaurant was a week ago. Cyclops told me every detail, of course: how delicious and **tender** the beef was, how delicious and tender Rob's lips were. They only need to stay together for

+++ to iron – bügeln +++ item – *hier:* Einzelheit +++ low-fat – fettreduziert +++ carbs – Kohlenhydrate +++ fancy – schick +++ tender – zart +++

another seven weeks. It doesn't exactly seem as though they're in the middle of a *Rosenkrieg. Aarrghhh*!

Someone taps me on the shoulder and I jump. I jump really high, like I'm **auditioning** for *High School Musical.* "Police!" says a – suspiciously Scottish sounding voice – behind me. "Stalking is illegal in London." Sam's **grinning**. "Emily, are you sick? You're actually on time tonight."

I'm still staring at Cyclops and Rob; Sam follows my gaze through the window. His face falls when he sees Chalk Farm's dream couple. "Oh no," he groans. "Let's go somewhere else."

It's a tragedy – there were chips in that café *with my name on them.*

It's not like White Out is the only café in the area. We're in Camden, for goodness sake, probably the hippest and liveliest part of London. It's full of cafés. It's full of chips. Still, it's a crying shame. I really felt like sitting in White Out tonight. I love it and haven't been in *this year*! I'm *sure* Amanda just went there to annoy me. She might have Rob's full attention but she's getting none from Miss Bardwell at the moment – she blames me for that, of course.

Sam and me walk, miserably, down Chalk Farm Road for a bit before finally ending up in an Internet café. We met here before, months ago, when I wanted Sam to do the "anti-Ed" website for us. It's not a very glamorous place for an important relationship conference.

+++ to audition – vortanzen +++ to grin – grinsen +++

There is at least one good thing about this café, though; it's quiet. It's mainly full of **geeks** and **tech heads** – like Sam – sitting **crouched** over their computers. But at least one person here is neither a geek nor a tech head. He's a handsome rugby god – it's Josh, Melissa's brother! He smiles over at Sam and me vaguely and then turns, **frowning**, back to his screen. He must be mailing Olga. How *is* Olga, I wonder?

I hear Sam ordering for us at the counter – *two glasses of Irn Bru and two plates of chips.* I sigh. I'd actually rather have a nice hot cup of tea. I don't dare tell Sam that. Irn Bru is the Scottish Coca Cola, apparently, and saying no to it would seem to be like saying: *I hate Scotland* or something.

There are a couple of tables which don't have computers at them and we take the only one free, in a corner. We sit down and talk a bit about Amanda and Rob first. Sam knows Rob, "… but not very well. He's in the year above me and he seems OK. I don't know what he sees in Amanda, honestly. Some boys just like the trashy types."

Sam looks at me in an odd way, half smiling. I don't exactly look trashy, right now, I'm sure that's what his half-smile means. I'm wearing an XXXL green woollen cardigan over my burgundy and yellow uniform. I must look like some giant aubergine, egg and lettuce salad or something. *Lecker!*

"It can't last …" I mutter. I mean Rob and Amanda,

+++ geek – Computerfreak +++ tech head – Tekkie (Technikexperte) +++ to crouch – hocken +++ to frown – die Stirn runzeln +++

of course. I don't want to tell Sam about my bet with Cyclops. I'm too ashamed. Instead, I repeat hopefully, "I mean, it can't, can it? What do you think are the chances they'll split up soon? I mean, five to one? Ten to one?"

Sam looks a bit **gloomy**. "I didn't know you were a gambler! I don't know. It's winter. Winter's boring. Rob will probably drop Cyclops in spring, when the sun comes out and the rugby season starts."

That might just be OK, I think, **anxiously**, as long as Rob finishes with Amanda exactly as the very first **daffodil** appears …

"Emily," says Sam a bit sharply. "Earth to Emily? Shall we talk about … us?"

Sam means Talk About Us, of course. It's time. He lets me do most of the Talking About Us, in fact. I try to make what I'm saying sound natural and cool. It's impossible, of course. Sentences like: "Let's just stay in the friends zone" can never really sound natural and cool, can they? Even worse, my voice is doing that odd thing that it does when I'm really nervous. *I sound German.* I'm **channelling** Onkel Dieter again: "in ze fwensah zone."

While I Talk About Us in my odd German-English voice, Sam just nods and drums with his fingers. Is he noticing how foreign I sound? He keeps looking **longingly** over at the computers. I'm sure he'd rather be playing *Grand Theft Auto* right now.

+++ gloomy – bedrückt +++ anxious – bange, ängstlich +++ daffodil – Osterglocke +++ to channel – umschalten auf +++ longing – sehnsüchtig +++

"So, emm, I think ve should just heng out togezah a bit und not lose each uzah." I finish, a bit weakly. I'm bright red. It's too hot in here. I should take my XXXL cardigan off, but I feel very shaky.

Sam says nothing for a moment. I can't tell what he's feeling, whether he's relieved or sad. Then he mutters softly, "Good call, Emily. I'd hate not to see you again too. I mean, it's the biggest cliché on the face of the planet, but let's try and stay friends ..."

He **bursts out laughing.** "You do realise you sounded *totally* German for a moment there, don't you? Really weird. It was a bit like Henry Kissinger telling me he wanted to be 'just friends' with me."

Sam looks so cute when he laughs, even when he's laughing *at* me. Oh, I could eat the face off him. That's slang for kissing here: *eating someone's face.* Charming, isn't it? But it's how I feel right now – *I'm hungry for him.*

Luckily, there's a nice big plate of chips in front of me now so I can just eat them instead. And it's nice to be able to say nothing for a bit. I'm still scared that the ghost of Onkel Dieter will break free again.

Now officially "just good friends", Sam and me make our way "home" to school. We walk and talk quickly. Sam tells me a bit of his news – his dad doesn't have a job but has been feeling better. Even so, Sam is sure that he'll go back to Scotland at the end of the school year. No, he hasn't told St Dougan's yet. Or *the band.*

It's clear that leaving the Kitty Gagarins is going to be

+++ to burst out laughing – in Lachen ausbrechen +++

the hardest thing to do. Sam's face and his voice both warm up when he talks about them: "I think we've really found our sound. We've been sending our CD around and we're going to put *Too Cool for School* as a download on our website - when it's finished." He looks a bit guilty. He's been working on the Kitty Gagarins site for ages.

"And we've got a couple of *killer* new songs." You can smell Sam's excitement, just for a second. Then his face falls again and he shrugs his shoulders. "It's only rock 'n' roll, you know? It's not diabetes or losing your job or your family needing you."

I nod hard. Of course. It's not really just rock 'n' roll, though, is it now? It's a ***passion.*** And what's life without your passions? I try to imagine how empty my life would be without photography. (It might, of course, be *exactly* that empty in around seven weeks, if Amanda

+++ passion – Leidenschaft +++

wins our little bet.) Music is an important part of our culture. Imagine life without music. Imagine there's no heaven.

What Sam needs is a sponsor. A **benefactor**, oops, I was dreaming again! Sam is so cold that he's hopping up and down – we're at the school gates. Saying goodbye is the first test of our new, official, platonic status and it's hell not to kiss him, naturally! Sam ends up just **punching** me – hard! – on the back, as though we were both in the rugby team and I'd just scored a goal. Or whatever you score in *rugby*.

As I walk back up the school **drive**, I do feel better, though. We've made the right decision. We'll get used to not kissing, I'm sure. And I'm starting to get a good feeling; the beginnings of a brilliant idea about who could help Sam.

First things first. It's time to sort things out with Maudie. I've been **avoiding** her ever since I made the world's most idiotic bet with Cyclops. Even though Maudie doesn't have a clue about it, I know in my heart that it's **affecting** our friendship. She asked me about Amanda and Rob the other day and I couldn't even open my mouth to reply.

I try to call Maudie first to see where she is, but she doesn't pick up her mobile. I dial Kim's number next – no answer there either. So I look in the Bloomsbury common room, where there's still no sign of them.

+++ benefactor – Wohltäter/in +++ to punch – klopfen +++ drive – Auffahrt +++ first things first – alles der Reihe nach +++ to avoid – aus dem Weg gehen +++ to affect – sich negativ auswirken auf +++

I'll have to keep hunting. The girls must be in one of their dorms. They don't actually share a room and I can only remember the number of Maudie's room – she's 1A, though I guess she's not exactly feeling *eins A* at the moment. I knock on the door and someone says something that sounds like "Yeah?", so I go in.

Maudie's sitting on her bed. I know it's her bed because there's a huge poster of Kurt Cobain above it. Maudie's a bit obsessed with him. She was born on the same day – April 5th 1994, if you're interested – he died. She feels like he's her *soulmate*, she told me once. Which seems a bit *weird*, if you ask me.

She's wearing her iPod, of course, and as she takes her headphones out, I can hear what she's been listening to. *What have I done to deserve this.* Oh no. Not again.

Maudie looks surprised to see me, but happy, too. "I'm glad you came over. I was just sitting here feeling a bit sorry for myself."

"Rob?" I ask and she nods. And then, it's suddenly just exactly the right time to **get things off my chest**. I tell Maudie all about the stupid bet with Amanda. All the **ridiculous** details: "I only *meant* to show her that she had no chance with Rob. Unfortunately ..." I hang my head in shame. Kurt Cobain looks at me sternly.

Maudie's face, for a moment, is an emotional traffic light: red with anger, then yellow with horror and finally green with, well, whatever the feeling is, it makes her laugh. "Oh Emily, you're a ***moron***. What if Cyclops really does win your camera?"

+++ to get things off one's chest – sich etwas von der Seele reden +++ ridiculous – lächerlich +++ moron – Depp, Schwachkopf +++

I forgot one very important thing there for a moment: Maudie's *nice.* That's why she's my friend. I'm forgiven. I join her on the bed and then we – don't be sick – hug and tell each other that we hate all boys, except 1) Kurt Cobain, 2) possibly Sam. Possibly.

School of Rock

So now that things are settled with Maudie, I can get back to thinking about how to help Sam. I've definitely got a plan. I'm dreaming about it in Maths the next school day: all those numbers, you can't help but think about money, can you?

It's obvious, isn't it? Money is the answer. I certainly can't help Sam with that but I know someone who could. Someone who already "sponsors" me. Someone who **prides herself on** being *eine Gönnerin der schönen Künste.*

I'm talking about the Queen Mother, of course. A woman who – *O-Ton, mein Vater – hat mehr Geld als Krösus.* She loves to go on and on about how she supports the arts – the usual things, ballet, opera, orchestras. So why not "**Pimp** my grandmother" and add rock musicians to that list!

I know what you're thinking. It's a mad idea, *natürlich.* But it might just work. I'm totally sure I can **persuade** the Queen Mother to help Sam. She wants to come here to Chalk Farm next week anyway. I got a let-

+++ to pride oneself on – sich etw. einbilden auf +++ to pimp – *hier:* aufpeppen +++ to persuade – überzeugen +++

ter from her only yesterday saying that she "missed me" and inviting herself for a visit.

"Missed me" – ha! I'm not fooled. The Queen Mother was **devastated** about my report card last term. She wants to talk to Miss Bardwell. I don't think the Queen Mother can understand how her darling "Connie" could possibly have been so cruel to her sort-of-darling granddaughter.

It's an excellent opportunity to put forward my "Sam Aid" **proposal** to her. Still, I have to be very careful. My report card said that I had been spending too much energy chasing the boys across the street. Asking my grandmother to give a lot of money to someone from St Dougan's might seem a bit *suspicious*. I have to come up with the right strategy.

I've got a couple of days to work one out. The Queen Mother will arrive here on Friday. She calls me to tell me her exact plans: she'll meet "Connie" first in the afternoon and have a quick chat in Latin with her. Then we'll go together to the hotel where she's staying – sorry, the *million dollar hotel* where she's staying – and have dinner there.

I had, of course, offered my grandmother the key to Nora's place: "You could stay there …" But she just exploded: "My dear Emily, I'm far too old to stay in a *commune*."

I think the Queen Mother really does imagine that Nora lives in some dirty *WG*, surrounded by **dope**-

+++ devastated – am Boden zerstört +++ proposal – Vorschlag, Antrag +++ dope – Haschisch +++

smoking Communists and stinky hippies. *Whatever.* She's only staying one night. She'll go straight back to Surrey on Saturday morning and will probably sleep for a week to **recover** from all the excitement of the *Hauptstadt.*

We have Art on Friday afternoons; our classroom looks out over the school gates and drive. So I get a bird's eye view of the Queen Mother arriving at our school by taxi and Miss Bardwell greeting her. I feel nervous that they'll be talking about me, but I'm *even more* worried that Miss Bardwell will say something about Nora. Oh, I feel sick.

But when I meet the Queen Mother and Miss Bardwell in the school foyer at 4.30 pm, they both seem pretty jolly. The Queen Mother smiles at me as I **approach** them; Miss Bardwell just has that odd emotion-free mask on. I heave a **sigh of relief.**

We say goodbye to Miss Bardwell and take a taxi to the QM's luxury twelve-and-a-half-star hotel. She really *is* in a good mood. "Miss Bardwell spoke quite positively about you," she says. "She said she thought you had potential …"

Potential to do what? Be a homeless **drug addict** one day? It's unbelievable. It's like this is "Second Life" and it's me who's putting words in the "Miss Bardwell" **avatar's** mouth. *I can control her.*

We arrive at the posh hotel, drop the Queen Mother's

+++ to recover – sich erholen +++ to approach s.o. – sich jmdm. nähern +++ sigh of relief – Seufzer der Erleichterung +++ drug addict – Drogenabhängige/r +++ avatar – virtuelle Person +++

posh bag and go to the posh dining room, which is full of posh people – I half-expect to see Marie Antoinette nodding to me across the room. Not that she'd have a head to nod, I suppose.

Grandma orders us the kind of meal that princes in Dubai might have every day but which I've never had in my life before: five tiny but super delicious courses! *Eat your heart out, Cyclops!*

Then I actually have a pleasant chat with the Queen Mother. She now has a new **hearing aid** and she doesn't *shout* at you like she used to, which is a relief in a restaurant as quiet and grand as this.

When we've finished eating, a funny thing happens. The Queen Mother says brightly, in her new gentle tone, "Actually, Emily, there's something I'd like to talk to you about …"

She says this at exactly the same time as I say brightly, "Actually, Grandma, there's something I'd like to talk to *you* about …"

Ladies first. The Queen Mother **kicks off**. And she gives me, well, maybe not the surprise of my *life* but certainly the surprise of the *year*. So far.

Do you know how this all started months ago? With me getting a phone call, standing half-asleep in the hall of our flat in Berlin and listening to the Queen Mother shouting at me, something about *a school year in London*!

It's a very different **setting** now. We're in a beautiful

+++ hearing aid – Hörgerät +++ to kick off – anfangen +++ setting – Situation +++

candle-lit restaurant, we're together, I'm not half-asleep. It's still **essentially** *déjà vu two*. I have – sort of – been here before: The Queen Mother offers to pay for me to spend another school year in London.

I am, honestly, shocked. Later, **reflecting on** it all, it was obvious that Grandma would do this, but I honestly hadn't even considered it. It was always clear to me: one school year in London and then back to Hermann-Hesse, Prenzlauer Berg, my family, my friends.

The Queen Mother has just turned everything on its head. She's smiling at me. She's had a glass or three of expensive white wine. She doesn't normally drink much and I wonder if she might be just a *tiny bit* drunk:

+++ essentially – im Wesentlichen +++ to reflect on – nachdenken über

"Emily, I'd like you to think about it. I know that it's not always been easy for you to be so far away from home. But I do truly believe it's been a character building time for you. The opportunities Chalk Farm School offers you are excellent. It's a once in a lifetime chance."

It's a *twice* in a lifetime chance, it seems. Grandma goes on and on and, of course, at some point it all becomes a monologue about everything Chalk Farm School gave *her*. This is fine because it lets me think quickly: It's the perfect chance. The Queen Mother is **willing to** pay for another year at school in London. I can say *thanks but no thanks* and then ask if perhaps she'd like to think about paying for a school year for someone else instead of me.

It's like a game of poker. Well, it might be. The only card game I know is *Mau Mau*, in fact. I'm just patiently waiting for the Queen Mother to take a breath – she won't actually stop talking for any other reason – so I can put my cards on the table.

I haven't really thought this through, of course. I haven't actually considered whether I *would* like to spend another year here or not. It's Sam I'm thinking of now. Even if I would *maybe* like to stay, Sam needs this more than me.

The Queen Mother pauses suddenly to take a sip from her wine glass – it's my **cue**. "Grandma," I say **eagerly**, "it's a very kind offer – really very kind. I just

+++ to be willing to – bereit sein zu +++ cue – Einsatz +++ eager – eifrig +++

don't believe it would be in my best interests to stay in London for another year. I don't want to be out of the school system in Germany for too long. I have to start thinking about my *Abi* ..."

The Queen Mother looks at me suspiciously. She doesn't like it when I use German words that she doesn't understand, so I explain quickly, "You know, my final school certificate."

"But you could do the IB here," **splutters** the Queen Mother. "It's recognised across the world. You could work or study anywhere with it!" (Boring additional information: IB = International Baccalaureat.)

"Right," I mumble slowly. True – but *Sam*! "The fact is, Grandma, there is someone else I know who would like an extra year at school here but can't afford it."

I tell her all about Sam. Every horrible detail, about his dad being ill and losing his job and them having no money to pay Sam's school **fees**. Then I say carefully, "And, Grandma, Sam's a musician of talent! He has a promising future in the ... music scene here in London."

The music scene in London. My grandmother thinks I mean with the London Symphony Orchestra or something.

"Which instrument does he play?" asks the Queen Mother, looking at me over the top of her crystal glass. She's actually listening to me – she *must* be drunk.

Grandma is obviously expecting me to say *oboe* or

+++ to splutter – hervorstoßen +++ fee – Gebühr +++

bassoon or something and when I say "drums" she's *not amused* for a moment. She looks at me as though I'd said *Leberwurst*. Then she laughs, "Oh, you mean *timpani!* **Kettle drums**."

"Errr, yes," I mutter. Well, Sam must play them, too, right?

A waiter appears. Sort of. He half-appears. The waiters are almost invisible here – exactly the way a good waiter should be, the Queen Mother always tells me. I think **fondly** of Mrs White, who couldn't be more *visible*. The ghostly waiter fills up the Queen Mother's wine glass and then is gone again. Or maybe not, as I can't actually see him anyway.

The Queen Mother now has a very serious expression on her face. "And, how, may I ask, do you know this young man? What did you say his name was – Samuel?"

She's remembering my report card. *So many boys, so little time.*

"We met at a concert," I say slowly. The Queen Mother's face **lights up**. I nearly laugh because I know exactly what's lighting her up. It's like there's a big window in her head. The only kind of concerts that the Queen Mother has experienced are classical ones, the kind where people clap by **rattling** their diamonds.

In her mind now, Sam's in a **dinner jacket** and has his hair **gelled** back. I'm wearing a 1950s style **debutante** dress and have my hair up in a **beehive**. "And this young

+++ bassoon – Fagott +++ kettle drums – Pauken +++ fond – liebevoll +++ to light up – sich aufhellen +++ to rattle – schütteln, rasseln mit +++ dinner jacket – Smoking +++ to gel – gelen +++ debutante – Debütantin +++ beehive – Dutt +++

man was playing at the concert?" I nod. It's all true so far, isn't it?

It's a very thoughtful Queen Mother that I'm now sitting opposite. "Samuel may be an excellent musician, Emily, but can you please tell me exactly why I should help him? And I do wish you would give more thought to another year here." She looks very, very sad suddenly.

"You should help Sam because he needs it," I say softly. "And, well, I …"

I honestly don't know if I want another year at Chalk Farm School or not. It just doesn't **seem likely** that the Queen Mother will pay for two poor teenagers to go through school here. I mean, even she's not *that rich*, is she?

Surprise – I'm wrong. Again. The Queen Mother really is *that rich* and she's ready to make a deal. The offer on the beautiful table in front of us is: *two for the price of one.* The Queen Mother will *think about* helping "Samuel, the young classical music student" if I, **in turn**, will *think about* giving Chalk Farm School another year of my life.

It's a *monster* dilemma. If I stay, Sam gets his fees paid. If I go back to Berlin, the **deal's off**. For a pensioner with *1,8 Promille*, she's actually pretty sharp, my grandmother.

I have time to make up my mind. The Queen Mother, of course, has already discussed things with "Connie":

+++ to seem likely – wahrscheinlich sein +++ in turn – im Gegenzug
+++ the deal is off – der Handel ist vom Tisch +++

"She'd be delighted if you stayed!!!" I have to decide by the middle of April. There is, of course, a massive waiting list for places at Chalk Farm School. The world is just full of parents who *hate* their daughters and can't wait to **get rid of** them, it seems. I was "lucky" last year, I now remember – I got the place of some girl who was ill. She **had a narrow escape**, that girl.

The Queen Mother and me agree that I'll go and visit her at The Grange for a couple of days in April – after Betti and Merle have left – to tell her about my decision. And then Grandma **wobbles** up the stairs, possibly helped by an invisible waiter, and I get in a taxi and go back to school.

Oh, man. I feel like I've just arrived here in London. It seems like only last weekend that I was in Broughton's, trying on my new uniform and feeling very, very ill. It seems like only last week that I was sitting down in the cafeteria and eating my first ever **beef olive** and feeling very, very ill. Now, already, I have to decide if I want a *zweite Portion* of it all.

+++ to get rid of s.o. – jmdn. loswerden +++ to have a narrow escape – gerade noch mal davonkommen +++ to wobble – schwanken +++ beef olive – Rindsroulade +++

Nora's back

My dad likes to say – likes to say too often – *Life is what happens to you while you're busy making other plans.* I think John Lennon might have said it before him, but you get the idea. It's the way I feel right now anyway. I'm trying to *plan, plan, plan.* I *plan* that I'll take a week to reflect on the Queen Mother's offer. But as it turns out, life will have other *plan, plan, plans* for me.

School goes on as "normal". Sort of. Whatever "normal" means this year. Miss Bardwell ignores me – and Amanda! – and generally acts a bit like Olga Petrova used to, staring out of the window a lot and sighing. Miss Bardwell's actually lost weight, too. She was always *too* thin, but now she looks as though, if you opened the classroom window, the wind could blow her away.

It's almost a bit *boring* with Miss Bardwell like this. There's no one to fight with right now. Amanda's so busy with Rob that I never see her. They seem to be **getting on** worryingly well, **incidentally**. They went ice skating at the weekend! Cyclops! Ice skating! Unbelievable.

Luckily, there is some big, better news this week: Nora

+++ to get on – sich verstehen +++ incidental – zufällig +++

will be back in London on Sunday! Great. We arrange that I'll meet her at her flat. She'll get in on Sunday morning so I'll stay in her flat on Saturday night and then we'll breakfast together. **Catch up**. I can't wait.

I end up phoning Sam to invite him over for Saturday night – platonically, OK? I'm desperate to tell him about my fantastic plan to keep him in London. But he said he couldn't make it: band practice. The Kitty Gagarins have finally set a date for their next concert. It will probably be *their last concert*. Sam's told the band that he's leaving at the end of the school year! "So April 6th, put the date in your Blackberry! It'll be a *legend*. I'll put you and your friends on the guest list."

I panic. "I need to see you before April," I mutter quickly.

This is a *disaster*. I hadn't considered the possibility that Sam might tell everyone he was going before I'd had a chance to let him know about the Queen Mother's deal. What do I do now? I suppose it won't matter. He can always just say he's changed his mind! Tell them it's a mystery benefactor. Something like that.

Sam suggests seeing a film later in the week. "It's "Student Night" on Tuesday," he laughs. "Half-price. And there's a Norwegian documentary about terrorism I'd like to see."

Fantastic! I was dying to know more about *both* Norway and terrorism! The cinema's not the best place to talk so I suggest meeting in the foyer and having a hot dog and a Coke first. I can just hear myself: *I'll stay if you*

+++ to catch up – nachholen +++

stay. I can see Sam's face: *he doesn't have to leave the band or me. He'll be* ***over the moon.***

The rest of Saturday night at Nora's place is heaven, actually. I have the TV control to myself – definitely no *Windswept Love*, that terrible soap that is always on in the common room – and eat a whole giant bag full of caramel covered popcorn. This makes me feel a bit sick. Not sick enough to stop me **making a decision**: I realise that I know what I'm going to do – I'll stay another year in London. For Sam. And educational reasons, of course.

There will just be one **condition** – either me or Cyclops moves out of dorm 3B. There's no way I'm spending another year locked up with that **maniac**. No way.

So I've got my plan. Now I just have to wait and see what life actually **has in store** for me.

In the morning I get up early: I'm *sooooo* excited about seeing Nora. This is a really bad idea. Nora said she'd be home by 12. *She said.* I forgot that Nora lives in her very own time zone and you have to add three hours to anything she tells you. So it's around 3, of course, when Nora does finally arrive. I'm bored out of my mind and I'm actually doing some Biology homework on genetics when she arrives. *That's* how bored I am.

Nora has a complicated story to tell about "getting

+++ over the moon – überglücklich +++ to make a decision – eine Entscheidung treffen +++ condition – Bedingung +++ maniac – Verrückte/r +++ to have in store – bereithalten +++

through **customs**" and "finding a taxi" but she's here at least. She looks good: she's brown – not as brown as Amanda, of course, but brown. She's thinner, too. "I had quite a nasty stomach infection," she says cheerfully. "Beirut Belly! So no curries for me for a while!"

She tells me something about her experiences in the Middle East but not much. She needs time to **process** it all, she says slowly. She walks over to the window. She's checking on her car: "It's still there, I hope! No one stole it? I forgot to look on the way up."

As she stands there in the light, Nora looks **x-ray** thin. Just like *you know who.* I don't know why I say what I say next. It just slips out: "Miss Bardwell's lost a lot of weight, too." *Why? Why do I say that*?

+++ customs – Zoll +++ to process – verarbeiten +++ x-ray – Röntgenstrahl +++

Nora's face falls immediately and she flashes a look at the answering machine. *37 calls* says the display. *98% of them are from Mr Michaels. He's crazy about you.*

Then Nora stares at me guiltily. "How is Connie?"

I shrug my shoulders. "Thin and miserable."

Nora looks back over at me. "Oh, Emily. I'm so sorry about it all. Ben thinks he's in love with me. It's nonsense, of course. He doesn't even *know* me. He keeps saying that breaking things off when we were young was the biggest mistake of his life."

"What about Miss Ba..." I begin and Nora sighs so hard that my hair actually *moves*, even though I'm sitting two metres away from her.

"Ben told me ..." Then Nora stops and looks at me very sternly. "This is all **confidential**, of course."

So, sorry, but I can't tell you what she told me about Miss Bardwell and Mr Michaels' relationship because it is, well, *confidential.* But if I were you, I would read between the lines. I'd read something like: *Mr Michaels was too scared of Miss Bardwell to break off their* ***engagement****.* You didn't hear that from me, of course.

I *can* tell you what Nora's going to do about Ben. This is not confidential. Here it is: *she's not interested.* "I did say we could just be friends – the old cliché! – but that never really works. I'll have to break off all contact with him. That's the only way. Emily! You look like you're going to cry! I never knew you cared about Miss Bardwell so much. Is that what's wrong?"

+++ confidential – vertraulich +++ engagement – Verlobung +++

Of course not. I don't care very much about Miss Bardwell. I'm sorry that she's suffering, but there's still no doubt that since she had her heart broken, my life's been a better place to be.

No, I'm thinking about what Nora has just said: *being friends never works.* She's right, of course. So what does that mean for Sam and me? *It never works, it never works.* There's an echo in my head. A bad one.

Nora says patiently, "Emily, what *is* the matter?" It's my turn to **reveal** to Nora why I'm really so sad. I tell her about Sam and all his problems at home, that he's leaving London. How happy I felt that we'd decided to be friends. How stupid it now seems.

Nora sighs a **mighty** sigh again. "Oh, Emily! I didn't mean *you and Sam*, I meant *Ben and me.* It might be possible for you two. Things are easier when you're younger. When there's no one else."

There's a long silence. I decide to tell Nora everything – all about my plan to help Sam, too. I'm so sure Nora will confirm that it's a brilliant idea of quiet genius that will let Sam stay in London and make amazing music.

Nora, however, isn't **impressed**. She thinks for a moment then says quietly, "Don't you think you should have asked Sam first if he wants help? I mean, he sounds like quite a proud guy. You *could* see the offer as **insulting. Charity** or something."

Oh. Insulting. Charity. I didn't think of any of those

+++ to reveal – verraten, enthüllen +++ mighty – *hier:* tief +++ impressed – beeindruckt +++ insulting – beleidigend +++ charity – Almosen +++

things. I can feel my lip wobbling. There's no way I'm crying again in front of Nora, though. I did that last time over Ed. It's too silly, to keep crying about boys. Boys. My life would be about 98% less complicated without them.

Nora's joined me on the sofa. "Emily, honestly, it's not that bad. It was a nice thought. Just be tactful. And remember, he might actually want to go home to his family."

"I know that," I say a bit **grumpily**. I do, I'm not stupid. But I can give Sam **options**, can't I?

Nora then looks at me in a strange way and says, "One more thing: if you do decide to stay, it should be because *you* want to. Don't let the Queen Mother – or me, or anyone – **blackmail** you. And don't just stay here because of a *boy*, Emily."

+++ grumpy – mürrisch +++ option – Wahlmöglichkeit +++ to blackmail – erpressen +++

Money Can't Buy Me Love

Because of a boy – no way. I'm not that stupid. Am I? Am I????

On Tuesday it's finally time to find out. Time to tell Sam about the Queen Mother's "offer". The **venue** is the Odeon, the same cinema at which we had our lovely, lovely Japanese film date. My "plan" is for us to talk about what the Queen Mother has offered for a bit over a Coke, then go in and see the Norwegian film. That was the *plan.*

What life has planned for us, however, is the following: Sam and me never actually make it inside the cinema. Over a hot dog and a drink in the foyer, I **mention** casually that the Queen Mother would be "happy" to sponsor Sam for the next school year. And then something very strange happens.

Instead of falling on his knees and thanking me for saving his brilliant rock career and giving our relationship a second chance, Sam goes completely nuts. ***Loco.*** He starts **smashing up** furniture and punching popcorn sellers. Not really, but as close as Sam could ever get.

+++ venue – Örtlichkeit +++ to mention – erwähnen +++ loco (span.) – verrückt +++ to smash up – zertrümmern +++

It's awful. I mean, Nora had warned me. I had thought it *possible* that Sam would say, "No thanks," but I didn't think he would tell me that I was an "**interfering** rich kid". "Rich?" That's worse than interfering!

"Sam," I say, looking round me nervously – everyone is staring at us. "I'm not rich, I mean, my grandmother would pay for me, too. She pays for me *now*, you know that."

Sam is bright red. "Yes, but she's your *grandmother*. Your *rich* grandmother from your *rich* family."

Sam's final words to me, before he storms out of The Odeon, are, "Thanks again but I'm not for sale. Money can't buy you love, Emily. Don't you know the song?" And I'm left sitting alone, more embarrassed than I've ever been in my life.

That went really well, don't you think?

Nora was right. It *was* an insulting offer. Sam really thought I was trying to get my grandmother to buy him for me, like he was a cow at a market or something. Disaster. Will he ever forgive me? Will I ever forgive myself?

I honestly did mean to be kind, but now I've ruined everything. Friendship with Sam – I can *forget it.*

I try to make peace with Sam over the next few days. After I've sent him five text messages, he finally replies: ***Leave me alone.*** So that's it. He hates me, it seems. It's completely over. Brilliant.

And **meanwhile** in a parallel universe, in the land of

+++ to interfere – sich einmischen +++ to leave s.o. alone – jmdn. in Ruhe lassen +++ meanwhile – in der Zwischenzeit +++

fairy-tale love – daffodils are blooming, the **snowdrops** are coming, the leaves are appearing on the trees. Spring is here and they've done it. On March 13th I am awoken at 6.30 am by the sight of Cyclops leaning into my face and the sound of her voice, saying, "It's our **anniversary** today, Emily. Eight weeks. Rob and me are going for a little dance tonight to celebrate. So, *you lose*, Hausmann. Hand it over, *loser*. Your camera, *loser*."

It's a nightmare. Maybe it really is? I'm so sleepy and the dorm is still dark. Then Amanda switches the light on and holds out her hands. It is real – awfully, painfully real.

The most **precious** thing on earth to me. *I have to.* I reach for it. I hand it to Amanda. It's awful. I've sold my **soul** – to the devil in sunglasses.

For a while, I wander round in shock. The shock lasts for about a day and then, unfortunately, I start to feel things again. What I feel most strongly is: *I want to go home.*

Really, I've had enough of London. Everything's turned sour. I'm sick of Cyclops, I've lost Sam forever. My mind is suddenly **made up**. There's no way I could ever spend another school year here. I simply have to survive the next two or three months … just stayin' alive. Just **killing time** till I can go back to Berlin. And maybe it's not too late with Sebastian. I'll definitely mail him this week.

+++ snowdrop – Schneeglöckchen +++ anniversary – Jubiläum +++ precious – wertvoll +++ soul – Seele +++ made up – *hier:* klar +++ to kill time – die Zeit totschlagen +++

The only thing I have to **look forward to** in the near future is the Easter holidays, some time off and a chance to show Betti and Merle round London. That will be fun, I hope. It had better be.

I've already got their trip all planned. We have to do the art galleries, of course. The Tate Modern is **a must see** – even though it will always make me think about the Kitty Gagarins photo shoot. I have to show Betti and Merle the **fleamarkets** in Camden – even though Camden Market always makes me think about Ed Stanton. Then there's White Out, of course – even though that was so special to Sam and me. And as for the Kitty Gagarins concert … oh, *I give up*! *Everything* in London **reminds** me **of** my failed relationships. Like I said – time to go.

I have to try and put on a brave face for Betti and Merle. Laugh through the tears. They mustn't know how terrible I feel. I've already told them about the Kitty Gagarins concert. They really want to go. I want to as well. It will be the last time I ever see Sam play – maybe the last time I *ever see Sam*. I'll just have to buy us some tickets. I can't expect Sam to still have us on the guest list now.

I **drift** through the next couple of weeks. I'm actually happy that we have **loads of** school work. It stops me missing Sam so much. Then, **out of the blue**, just as I've

+++ to look forward to – sich freuen auf +++ a must see – etwas, das man gesehen haben muss +++ fleamarket – Flohmarkt +++ to remind s.o. of sth. – jmdn. an etwas erinnern +++ to drift – sich treiben lassen +++ loads of – eine Menge +++ out of the blue – aus dem Nichts +++

given up and said goodbye to London forever in my head and my heart, some strange things happen.

The first of these is that I actually get a text message from Sam: *Rob wants your number!! gave it to him, hope that's ok. what's going on?*

What *is* going on? I've never even met Rob. Why would *he* want my number? But sure enough, I get a text message from Rob about half an hour later, asking if I can meet him at the school gates.

It's **intriguing.** I have no idea why Rob would want to see me. Perhaps he wants to punch me for being nasty to his girlfriend? I've hardly spoken to Cyclops in the last couple of weeks, though. It can't be.

It doesn't take me long to **work it out**. Rob is standing at the gates already when I arrive for our mysterious rendezvous. He's carrying a camera over his shoulder – **hang on**, he's carrying *my* camera over his shoulder! He looks a bit angry about something.

When he sees me, he holds my Pentax out to me straight away. "This is yours, I believe?"

I nod **dumbly**, taking my camera. It feels amazing. I stare at Rob, wide-eyed. He looks back at me. "You lost it in a bet, is that right? Wasn't that a bit stupid? Sam tells me you're really into photography."

I don't say anything. I want to ask, *but how did you get it back from Cyclops?*

Rob says **grimly**, "If you're wondering how I got it back from Amanda – she gave it to me, that's how. She

+++ intriguing – verblüffend +++ to work sth. out – etw. herausfinden +++ Hang on – Warte mal +++ dumb – *hier:* stumm +++ grim – grimmig +++

said it was my break-up present. She thought it was really funny. She said she didn't need me any more and she certainly didn't need this camera – so we were perfect for each other. Was this some stupid game between the two of you?"

"No," I mutter quickly. "Cy… I mean, *Amanda* and me don't play games. We don't actually, you know, *like* each other."

Rob stares at me. He doesn't really look like someone who's just been dumped, I have to say. He doesn't seem broken or depressed. He does seem a bit *relieved.*

"Are you OK?" I say. I mean, if I were him I'd be ecstatic, but I *suppose* he must be hurting a bit inside somewhere. He's just been dumped. That's never nice. Is it?

Rob looks surprised. "Me? I'm fine. The rugby season starts again soon."

Boys. They're so **predictable**.

And I suppose it's also predictable that Sam calls me later. He's a bit uneasy. "I just wanted to know what Rob wanted your number for." He actually sounds a tiny bit **jealous**. It can't be true, of course.

I finally tell Sam the story about my crazy gamble with Amanda and there's a shocked silence at the other end of the line. "Emily, you're mad. You nearly lost your camera forever."

"I know," I say **glumly**. "Sometimes I don't think

+++ predictable – berechenbar +++ jealous – eifersüchtig +++ glum – mürrisch +++

things through. I just say what seems like a good idea at the time."

I'm talking about my bet with Cyclops, but I could just as easily mean offering Sam my grandmother's money. He knows that.

There's another long pause. Then Sam finally mumbles, "Emily, you have a good heart. Listen. Your offer was kind. Really. I was **rude**. And maybe I should have thought about it for a bit longer …"

I can't believe it. "Oh, right, yes, OK," I **stutter**. *Is he saying that he'll think about staying on in London?* I'm confused.

Sam changes the subject: "You're still on the guest list for the concert. *Emily Hausmann plus four.* Your two friends from Berlin and Maudie and Kim, right?"

"Kim won't come," I say. "But thanks, that's great."

"See you all there then!" laughs Sam. I could be wrong – it wouldn't, as I'm sure you know, be unusual – but I think he sounds hopeful.

It's time to be a *Berliner* again. The school holidays have begun at Chalk Farm. I say goodbye to everyone in dorm 3B: Melissa – off to ride around in circles and **shovel** horse *Schiete* for two weeks. Becks – off to hockey camp for two weeks of *physical pain.* Amanda – off to Ibiza for two weeks of working on her tan. And hopefully some kind of physical or mental pain. Any kind.

I'm sure Cyclops has noticed that my camera is back again at my bedside but neither of us have said anything

+++ rude – gemein +++ to stutter – stottern +++ to shovel – schaufeln

about it. I can't decide whether she knew that Rob would give it back to me or not. I don't care that much suddenly.

I say *Bon Voyage* to Kim (off to the Dordogne with her family). I even say a quick goodbye to Miss Bardwell, who is off on **sabbatical** for the rest of the term to a "spiritual **retreat**". To *find herself*, according to her cousin's boyfriend's hamster or whoever. *Find herself?* That's a scary thought. I don't want her to *find herself!* I like the fact that she's *lost herself.*

Exhausted from saying *goodbyegoodbyegoodbye* all the time, I **stagger** to the airport to pick up Betti and Merle. I'm so excited. I can't believe the girls have finally made it here to London. We've planned it for so long – we'll stay at Nora's. We've talked about it for so long and they've dreamt about it for so long. Now, finally, here they are! *Live! Die Mädels!*

They're walking towards me in the arrival hall, pulling their suitcases behind them. I suddenly feel guilty as I realise that I borrowed Merle's beautiful vintage red case when I came to London all those months ago. I notice now that she has another nice one with her, an olive green one, which also looks vintage. Betti has her super business-like Samsonite case with her, the one that Merle always says makes her look as if she's on her way to an *EU Agrarwirtschaftsgipfel.*

I run over to them and hug them. I've brought them each a single pink rose, too, German style. (British peo-

+++ sabbatical – unbezahlter Urlaub +++ retreat – Rückzug +++ to stagger – taumeln +++

ple don't greet each other with flowers like we Germans do. They're not as nice.) Merle does what she always does in these situations and bursts into tears. "Ich habe dich so vermisst!" she bubbles. "Kann kaum glauben, dass wir hier sind!"

Betti probably can't believe it either – this is only her second time abroad, I know – but she's playing things cool, *wie immer*. She's acting as if going abroad is something that happens all the time to her. *EU Gipfel und so.*

But she does hug me, too, and grin. "Mein Schatz, London! Do we have to speak English miteinander now oder wie?"

We take a bus to Nora's. Merle can't shut up and shrieks and screams at everything we see through the window, even things like *süße englische Briefkästen*! "Wäre schön, wenn man sie ab und zu mal ausschalten könnte," mutters Betti **under her breath**, **yawning**. "Bin jetzt seit sieben Stunden mit ihr unterwegs und sie hat *nicht einmal* aufgehört zu reden."

It's already six o'clock when we arrive at Cleveland Street. The girls are impressed by the flat, but we don't have time to really look around. We've only got time to **get changed** before we pick Maudie up and go to the Kitty Gagarins concert. While we get dressed and put on a bit of make-up, I finally tell the girls about the Queen Mother's offer. They are shocked. "Noch ein Jahr, Emily! Wir halten es nicht aus!" **wails** Merle.

+++ under one's breath – flüsternd +++ to yawn – gähnen +++ to get changed – sich umziehen +++ to wail – jammern +++

This is always the point where Betti would usually say something wise and pragmatic. She doesn't: instead, her phone buzzes with a new message. She reads it, **giggles**, goes red and texts something back. She doesn't say anything about me staying or not staying in London. Weird.

I stare at her. I'm waiting for her at least to say who the message was from, as she also usually does, but she doesn't. So I stare at Merle and Merle winks and then giggles, "Ach komm, Betti – sag es ihr!"

And then I get the strangest news I've heard in, ooh, a couple of weeks probably. Betti – pragmatische, **sensible** Betti is going out with *Lars-Christoph Schmid*. Her Gothic stalker. It seems the Elvish love letters finally **paid off**.

I don't know what to say. I mean, Lars-Christoph is actually a sweet guy – but he's a *Goth*. Betti is an *anti*-Goth. She dresses a bit like a *Buchhalterin*. A hip *Buchhalterin* but **still**. It's like the sun dating the moon. Betti just says **cryptically**, in a very un-Betti way, "Du, ich kann es auch nicht erklären, aber irgendwie – ich mag ihn."

This relationship, of course, breaks about every rule in Betti's *Top-Liebestest*: *Habt ihr gemeinsame Interessen? usw.* I'm **stunned**. Betti just blushes. "Ich weiß … lass es mal."

Wir *lassen es mal* and pick up Maudie at Camden underground station. She looks terrific in a long black **lace** dress. (Like the kind of girl, in fact, who might date

+++ to giggle – kichern +++ sensible – vernünftig +++ to pay off – sich bezahlt machen +++ still – trotzdem +++ cryptic – rätselhaft +++ stunned – fassungslos +++ lace – Spitze +++

Lars-Christoph Schmid.) Maudie's really friendly to Betti and Merle. And Betti and Merle's English is actually pretty good, even though – don't *ever* tell her because she'd cut my **throat** – Betti does sound a *tiny bit* like Herr Eisenhardt, our English teacher back at Hermann-Hesse. And that's not totally a good thing.

We find the **community** centre where the Kitty Gagarins are playing. It's a great feeling to be on the guest list and we're nicely and rock 'n' roll in our timing, too – the band are coming on stage as we arrive. Ed Stanton appears first.

"Ooooh lecker," says Merle as Ed walks on. "Der ist doch *süüüüüüüß.*" Betti gives Merle one of "Betti's black looks". "Oh nein!" gasps Merle. "Natürlich. Habe grad nicht dran gedacht, Emily, Verzeihung!"

Merle then spends the rest of the evening telling me how süüüß Sam is, *noch viel hübscher als auf deinen Bildern/definitiv cool.* It almost gets annoying after a while to be honest.

The band plays a short **set** – "We don't have that many songs yet!" grins Steve – but three **encores**. Then they come back onto the stage one last time, with their arms around each other. They **bow** and I realise what they're going to say.

It's Ed who speaks: "Thanks so much. This was actually our final concert tonight in our **current line up**. Sam Reid, our drummer" – Sam takes another tiny bow,

+++ throat – Hals +++ community – Gemeinde +++ set – Abfolge von Songs +++ encore – Zugabe +++ to bow – sich verbeugen +++ current – aktuell +++ line up – Zusammensetzung +++

looking a bit tense – "will be leaving the band in summer. He's going back to Scotland and we wish him well."

Ed continues, "But the band will go on. We're looking for new drummers right now …" I've switched off. Sam's *definitely leaving. Definitely.*

Stop Making Sense

Then they're gone. It's terrible. Everyone looks shocked, even Maudie, Betti and Merle, who all knew that Sam *might* leave. *What happened to thinking about the Queen Mother's offer again?*

The hall is suddenly really quiet. The lights have gone up and everyone is just standing around, **blinking** hard. Maudie looks at me: "He's really leaving, eh?"

I nod. I don't know what to say. Then, suddenly Merle gasps! "*Guck mal!*" she says and then stops. I turn and there's Sam, still looking hot and sweaty. "Hi," he mumbles quietly, "I just wanted to say hello to the Berliners."

Sam shakes hands with Betti and Merle – their eyes **sparkle**. He asks them a bit about how they're finding London and compliments them on their English. He's absolutely charming. Finally he turns to me and says politely, "Listen, can I have a word with you alone?"

Betti winks at me and mutters, "*Sei vorsichtig, Mädel!*" I try to ignore her. Sam takes me by the arm, **firmly**, but not, you know, *aggressively* firmly and leads me backstage.

+++ to make sense – sinnvoll sein +++ to blink – blinzeln +++ to sparkle – funkeln +++ firm – fest +++

He takes out a key and opens a door – to the equipment room, it seems. Sam's **drum kit** and the bands' guitars are all already there, along with the **speaker** system. "This is all getting picked up later. Steve's brother's got a van. We're having a bit of an after-show party tonight. You know, the last concert."

The last concert. I hang my head and Sam suddenly bursts out emotionally, "I'm sorry, I should have told you first that I was definitely leaving. The band were really pushing me to make a decision, though, and it just …"

"… slipped out," I mutter. I know the feeling.

Sam looks at me seriously. "I want to say how sorry I am. I've been feeling terrible for weeks. The offer you made me was really kind, no question. But I just can't accept it. I've never even met your grandma. I can't take your family's money – they'd never respect me."

"*They don't respect me either,*" I mumble and Sam laughs. "It's still not really the point is it? The point is that people need me somewhere else. And those people are more important to me than the band or the school …"

Or me, I think sadly. More important than *me.*

I don't say that, I just I nod. I'm actually not **keen on** hanging around here much longer. I just want this over, this strange scene in this dark cupboard. It's sort of goodbye, I'm realising. It's the holidays again, Sam will be off up north and I won't see much of him, I'm sure, when he gets back.

+++ drum kit – Schlagzeug +++ speaker – Lautsprecher +++ to be keen on sth. – auf etw. Lust haben +++

Then Sam says, "But I think you should accept your grandmother's offer, I really do." And he tells me all the reasons why he thinks I should stay here in London. What an amazing city it is. How great Maudie and Kim are. What a good school Chalk Farm is.

His voice is suddenly more nervous: "And London is a bit nearer to Scotland than is Berlin. 414 miles. 667 kilometres to Glasgow. I looked it up. You could come and visit. It's only a few hours on the train, really."

You could say, of course, that Berlin and Glasgow are also only a few hours flying time from each other, but I don't. I'm too busy trying to work out what Sam means. Does he mean: *Come and see the sights of Scotland and I'll show you around as a friend?* Or does he mean: *Let's stay together, somehow*? He can't mean that. He can't. It wouldn't make any sense.

It *doesn't* make any sense. What Sam does next makes *even less* sense. He takes me in his arms and kisses me so hard that I nearly fall backwards onto his drum kit.

I don't have any idea how long we stay in the equipment room. If you told me we'd been in there for eight months, three weeks and a day, I'd just nod and say *right.* I'm totally lost in kissing Sam, in whispering to him and trying to understand just what *is* going on. All I **manage** to understand is this: Sam has missed me and he wants us, somehow, to try to stay together. Long distance love.

Sam's got it all planned. He already has a weekend job

+++ to manage – etw. schaffen +++

lined up in Glasgow, working in the computer shop of the friend of a friend. He'll do that every Saturday, with one day off a month. That's when he would come down to London and see me: "It's not *that* expensive."

I agree to what he's offering me. I'm not proud. I'll take Sam **on any terms**. And though I said I'd had enough, deep down, I don't believe I have. These have been the most exciting seven or eight months of my life, these London months. I can't imagine leaving it all behind in a few weeks. Something tells me that there's more excitement, more drama and more *love* to come here on the island. *Don't stay for a boy*, Nora said, and I won't. But I will stay for *love* – isn't there a difference? *Sort* of?

"Sam," I whisper, "I'll stay."

+++ lined up – geregelt +++ on any terms – unter jeder Bedingung +++

Sam laughs. He looks relieved. "You're really sure you want us to be together? I mean, we've got the next few weeks of term and then summer holidays. You could come to Scotland then. Or we could always go and see Mr Michaels in Uganda. Did you hear that he's taken a teaching job there? He's leaving, too, at the end of the year."

Uganda. Maybe Mr Michaels thinks it's the kind of place that Nora will end up in from time to time. Speaking of time – it's now "time" to find the others. Sam looks uneasy. "I have to go to the after-show party. I'd love you to come, but I suppose you won't because of …"

Ed. It's true. I don't feel much like talking to Ed Stanton. On the other hand, why not? I mean, what happened with the Babe Blog was *centuries* ago. Or it feels that way.

Then Sam grins. "There's another reason you might want to come. Something I've been meaning to tell you. Just between you and me, I think Matt might have his eye on Maudie."

"No way," I say, gasping. I can't believe it. Matt, the band member – there's always one, isn't there? – that you never really notice. Now I think about Matt, though, he *is* totally cute.

I laugh. "I'll go and get the others then, shall I?" and Sam grins. "I was hoping you'd say that. And we've got loads of chicken salad." I groan. Ed Stanton and his *chicken* ***addiction.***

+++ addiction – Abhängigkeit +++

Sam kisses me again and then I **float off**, back into the concert hall. I see the girls straight away. I must have been gone for ages, truly, because they're almost the only ones left in the place. The three of them are sitting up on the stage, laughing loudly about something. I knew they'd get on. Berlin meets London – and it works.

I'm wondering how to tell them about Sam but, of course, when they see me they start laughing even more loudly and Maudie **yells,** "It's written all over your face, Hausmann! Congratulations – I suppose you sorted everything out?"

I just go red. And then I say firmly, "Yes, I did. It's all sorted."

+++ to float off – wegschweben +++ to yell – rufen +++

Bei Thienemann von Joanna Thompson in der Reihe »Freche Mädchen – Easy English!« ebenfalls erschienen:

Girls' School – *England Calling*
Girls' School – *The Ed Affair*
Girls' School – *Season of Love*

Thompson, Joanna:
Girls' School – Stand by your Sam
ISBN 978 3 522 50088 3

Reihengestaltung und Gesamtausstattung: Birgit Schössow
Innentypografie: Marlis Killermann
Schrift: Minion und LTT Tapeside
Satz: KCS GmbH, Buchholz/Hamburg
Reproduktion: Medienfabrik, Stuttgart
Druck und Bindung: Friedrich Pustet, Regensburg

5 4 3 2 1° 09 10 11 12

www.thienemann.de
www.frechemaedchen.de